peace

peace

Steps to Achieving Happiness Through
Acts of Love, Compassion, Kindness,
Tolerance, and Forgiveness

tsem rinpoche

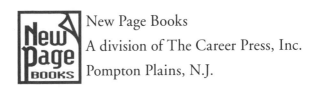

New Page Books
A division of The Career Press, Inc.
Pompton Plains, N.J.

PEACE
TYPESET BY KARA KUMPEL
Cover design by Fang Chyi Chang
Printed in the U.S.A.

To order this title, please call toll-free 1-800-CAREER-1 (NJ and Cana-da: 201-848-0310) to order using VISA or MasterCard, or for further information on books from Career Press.

The Career Press, Inc.
220 West Parkway, Unit 12
Pompton Plains, NJ 07444
www.careerpress.com
www.newpagebooks.com

Library of Congress Cataloging-in-Publication Data
Tsem Tulku, Rinpoche, 1965- author.
Peace : steps to achieving happiness through acts of love, compassion, kindness, tolerance, and forgiveness / by Tsem Rinpoche.
pages cm
Previously published: Petaling Jaya, Selangor, Malaysia : Kechara Media & Publications, 2009.
Includes index.
ISBN 978-1-60163-353-8 -- ISBN 978-1-60163-407-8 (ebook) 1. Peace--Religious aspects--Buddhism. 2. Dharma (Buddhism) I. Title.

BQ4570.P4T74 2014
294.3'444--dc23

2014036119

DEDICATION

"Me with Rinpoche—what merits did I have, to have my path cross with Rinpoche. That I can do Dharma work and share modern day Dharma to the world. Rinpoche has said many times, through a keyboard and a computer we can change so many people's lives. Thank you, Rinpoche, for a precious opportunity."

—**JUSTIN RIPLEY**, 23 August 2011

We dedicate this book to the memory of our dear Dharma brother, Justin Ripley, who has contributed to the spread of H.E. Tsem Rinpoche's teachings in more ways than one. He played an integral part in the growth of the Kechara Buddhist organization through his many talents, from volunteering in the soup kitchen to his extensive technical work on the Internet. Although he is no longer with us, we will always remember his enormous capacity for love, and the heart of peace and kindness he shared with so many. We look forward to meeting him again...

CONTENTS

His Eminence Telo Rinpoche

It is a great honor for me to have the opportunity to write this Foreword to the teachings of Tsem Rinpoche. Tsem Rinpoche has come a long way from the suburbs of New Jersey, USA. He hitchhiked his way across the United States to Los Angeles, just to study the Dharma that Lord Buddha taught us. He lived next to a cowshed in Gaden Monastery, south India, so that he could be close to his Guru, listen to the precious teachings and serve him in return for learning the Dharma. Now, he lives and works in the heart of Malaysia, only with the intention to do good and serve the community by spreading the Dharma—or the truth, as I would say. I call the Dharma the truth because the teachings of Lord Buddha are based on reality—the reality of the world that we live in.

Of course, from the materialistic point of view, there have been dramatic changes from the time of Buddha's existence but the one thing that has never changed is the human desire to be happy and to be free from any suffering. When we ask any human on this planet, "What is the purpose of life?" we get many different answers. Very rarely would a person say that the purpose of life is to be happy. Usually, a person who answers that the purpose of life is to be happy is one who has done some soul searching and follows some ethical principle or religion.

A question that is asked frequently is, "How do we achieve Happiness?" and it is asked as if it is a kind of souvenir we can buy from a store or give to someone as a present. But that is not the case. Tsem Rinpoche guides us here, throughout this book, on how we can achieve Happiness. This advice arises not just because Buddha said so, or dictated that this is how things should be done. Tsem Rinpoche guides us using what he learned from years of practice—mentally, physically and psychologically. This book is the result of the compassion, kindness, love and patience of Tsem Rinpoche.

One may ask where all this love and compassion came from. It did not arise naturally. If that was the case, then there would not be any wars or suffering that we all face in today's society. As humans, we are born with all these good qualities—such as love, compassion, kindness, tolerance and forgiveness—but we fail to utilize them in our daily lives because our negative emotions take over, dominating the human brain. We are all intelligent enough to distinguish between the negative and the positive but we are always in denial and fail to utilize the good qualities that are within us.

At the same time, we never feel embarrassed to show off our external material wealth which is, in reality, impermanent—like our lives. Actually, that material wealth is often created out of narrow-mindedness, self-centeredness and ignorance. What we are ignorant about is the fact that we carry many good qualities within ourselves but don't know how to share that wealth of goodness with the rest of the world.

I don't believe people when they say, "I am nobody and I can't make a difference in the world." Change starts from somewhere and it does not fall from the sky. Change is YOU. You are the one that can change and make a difference in other people's lives. This starts from teaching your own children, friends and family the good qualities of life; it goes on and on to future generations.

The only way to pass on the good qualities is by learning the Dharma, or the truth, just as a math teacher teaches us how to solve math problems in our classroom. Look upon Buddha as the doctor, his teachings as the medicine and Tsem Rinpoche as the nurse who shows you how to cure your disease by taking the right medicine. I am sure there is a cure to anything or any suffering we face in today's world. And, in this book there is a dose of such a cure that can lead you to liberation from any suffering. I am sure you will share this dose with others whom you love and cherish in your daily lives.

Telo Tulku Rinpoche
Shadjin Lama (Supreme Lama) of Kalmyk Republic
Moscow, August 2009

Datuk Dr. Victor Wee

Many of us, caught up in the secular world, are driven by ambition. We live our lives to achieve big dreams, earn big money and solve big problems when they arise. This is what we would like to do. But in the process of getting there, we face anxieties, frustrations, disappointments and "politics."

Every arena, workplace, family and community has its own politics. These "people problems" don't just exist among politicians. They exist anywhere there are people and we just have to deal with them.

How do we handle these people problems? We may try persuasion, diplomacy and "soft talk." When that fails, we may turn to other methods, such as anger, deception, manipulation, threat or even violence, to deal with our problems. Many of us are guilty of this, whether in a mild or extreme form. When confronted with frustration, we may even want to find an escape in religion, thinking that isolation and asceticism will calm our minds and take us away from dealing with "real life."

Yet deep down inside, we know that these methods to deal with our problems are really not the answer. They may be palliatives to make us feel better for a while but are never the real solutions. It takes a lot more effort to get through the trials and tribulations of life!

This book by H.E. Tsem Rinpoche is a wonderful, concise collection of teachings that show us exactly how to navigate through life's problems and yet achieve the wonderful balance, the "Middle Way." We should start where we are. I am extremely happy to see a book like this in Malaysia. We are a country that can boast strong cultural diversity and inter-ethnic harmony—the spiritual element, when put into practice, can contribute further to peace and happiness among our friends, colleagues, family and fellow Malaysians. It will forge stronger relationships everywhere.

Happier people mean happier neighborhoods, happier nations, happier regions and, eventually, world peace. Every little bit helps—finding solutions to every problem in the world begins with each of us, right where we are.

With folded hands, I thank Tsem Rinpoche for his straightforward, down-to-earth, yet profound advice that will apply to every one of us, at every level, no matter what we're doing. I hope it will make you feel as light and joyful as it has made me.

Datuk Dr. Victor Wee
Former Chairman, Tourism Malaysia
Malaysia, August 2009

ACKNOWLEDGMENTS

All of us involved in the production of this book would like to thank our Lama, His Eminence Tsem Rinpoche, for his constant guidance and teachings, which have inspired much joy and peace in beings everywhere.

The production of this book would not have been possible without the contribution and support of many.

HIS EMINENCE TSEM RINPOCHE:
A SHORT BIOGRAPHY

Beloved for his unconventional, contemporary approach to Dharma, H.E. Tsem Rinpoche brings more than 2,500 years of Buddhist wisdom and teachings to the modern spiritual seeker by connecting ancient worlds with new people, cultures, attitudes and lifestyles.

A Mongolian-Tibetan heritage, a childhood in Taiwan and in the United States of America, intensive monastic studies in India and now the Spiritual Guide of the Kechara organization in Malaysia—these are but some of the many facets that contribute to Tsem Rinpoche's unique ability to effortlessly bridge the East and the West. His teachings bring the Dharma to our everyday lives, and in doing so, he is able to bring the ancient time-honored Buddhist philosophies and practices into the 21st century.

Tsem Rinpoche has been strongly inclined towards Dharma since his early childhood, and has studied under many great Buddhist masters of the Tibetan tradition. Tsem Rinpoche eventually went on to receive his monastic education at Gaden Shartse Monastery, currently located in Mundgod in South India.

Following the advice of his beloved Guru, H.H. Kyabje Zong Rinpoche, Tsem Rinpoche took his vows as a monk from H.H. the Dalai Lama and joined Gaden Shartse Monastery when he was in his early twenties. His two preceding incarnations, Gedun Nyedrak and Kentrul Thubten Lamsang Rinpoche, had also studied at the original Gaden Shartse Monastery when it was then located in Tibet. There, they obtained Geshe Lharam degrees before completing their studies at Gyuto tantric college.

Gedun Nyedrak went on to become the lead chanter and, later, abbot of Gaden Monastery, while Kentrul Rinpoche brought the Dharma to the laypeople of the Phari district of Tibet. The tremendous and virtuous work of his previous lifetimes can perhaps be reflected again in Tsem Rinpoche's present-day activities in Malaysia, where he continues this selfless practice of teaching vast numbers of non-monastic communities in places where the Dharma has just begun to bloom.

During his nine years in Gaden, Tsem Rinpoche was involved in extensive charitable works including building schools for refugee children in India, building dormitories and upgrading living conditions for the monastic community, and providing long-term assistance to the poor lay community of Mundgod.

Now, based in Malaysia, Tsem Rinpoche continues this immense work to benefit many. Through creative and engaging approaches, Tsem Rinpoche continuously shares new methods of bringing happiness and relief to people from all walks of life, regardless of their religious faith. Tsem Rinpoche also maintains close contact with Gaden Monastery; through his constant practice of generosity and with a deeply altruistic motivation, he continues to frequently sponsor Gaden's work and activities.

Be inspired by H.E. Tsem Rinpoche's work and life and share in his personal views, thoughts and news on his blog at **tsemrinpoche.com.**

EDITOR'S INTRODUCTION

The beginnings of this book started a few years ago when I was transcribing a teaching called "Bring Dharma Home," from which several chapters in this volume have now been extracted. There, as in the chapter "Peace begins even though everyone around you is a nightmare," H.E. Tsem Rinpoche gives a wonderful, detailed "visualization" where we imagine preparing an extensive, beautiful retreat hut in the Himalayas. We fly there with the one person who irritates every cell in us, leave them in the hut with promises that the retreat will give them good luck, lock the door and speed back home in our helicopters.

"And then they're gone," says Rinpoche. "Those monster partners and friends are in retreat. We never have to hear their voices again, we never have to listen to them rant and complain…no more nagging, no more arguments, and no more weird conversations or ideas. Nothing. Just us! Wouldn't that be fun?"

"Just think about that. Would that be easier or would transforming ourselves be easier? The things that bother us about that person are real. But wouldn't it be easier if we just change ourselves?"

And just like that, we are taken off on a different journey into the Himalayas where the heart of ancient Buddhist wisdom reveals the transformative secrets we need to learn in order to change ourselves.

In reality, the second journey is not that much easier. It is difficult to traverse that path of self-transformation and change. In the first place, we think, why should we change? Things are fine just as they are. Changing anything in our comfort zone is distracting, difficult and even painful.

Then again, we realize eventually that staying in a comfort zone—with its hang-ups and conflicts—is far more painful, and that pain lasts far longer. The elusive, endless search for solutions to our problems often leads us into further frustrations; or we jump into a heady mix of distractions. Therapy, counselling, sports, relationships, money and business are merely fast fixes for all the ailments that rub up against each other in our hearts and heads, but soon enough, we find ourselves right back where we started.

The teachings compiled in this book with its simple title show us that the vast and faraway concept of peace itself is really right there in front of us; in the last place we would look.

While we search the far corners of the world for solutions and ideas and quick-fixes, it comes down to the simple fact that it is all up to us to start with what we have. Every one of us has that individual power to take that first step—out of our self-absorbed little worlds and into the rest of the world—to create a real difference in the lives of others. Rinpoche teaches us that undoubtedly, along the journey, we will also find little bonuses—happier truths for ourselves and the way we live our lives!

There is a Buddhist teaching that questions whether it would be easier to pave the whole world with leather so our feet will not be hurt by pebbles and dirt, or to wear a pair of shoes when we go out. Any logical person would immediately think that was a silly question—of course we should wear shoes! But we live out that metaphor in everything we do—we expect the whole world to be "paved" to suit our delicate sensibilities and emotions—when we should just make that small effort of "wearing shoes" and take the responsibility to create positive change.

Some readers may discover that certain chapters in this book shake them up and make them feel uncomfortable because all Rinpoche seems to do is point out failings. Other chapters offer wonderful antidotes; colorful yellow brick roads that can be softly stepped on. Actually, many chapters are all one and the same teaching—recognizing faults, failings and difficulties is just as significant as the subsequent steps we take to transform adversity into something positive.

The next realization that might surprise us is that each chapter is relevant to our lives. At first glance, we may think that the "problems" highlighted in these teachings do not have anything to do with us—we are not that kind of person, we do not have those sorts of conflicts and we do not do those kinds of things. Upon closer inspection, every one of us will soon recognize ourselves in each of the scenarios presented in these teachings; perhaps not exactly, but we'll certainly spot some twisted variation of ourselves there!

Sometimes, all we need to do is consider how we might react within given situations, and we will realize that we would react just as Rinpoche has "predicted" we would.

We are not as goody-two-shoes as we thought we were. Even if we were, the chapters of this book show us how to deal with people who are not. And it is quite inevitable that we will come across these people at some point in our lives. The relevance of these teachings lies in this fact: that we will always come face to face with problematic situations and difficult people. The candid advice given between the pages of this book can be applied to every moment of our daily lives.

Rinpoche's teachings bring us back to ourselves—they give us the rare opportunity to take a moment away from all the clutter that surrounds us and look at where we are right now. And, as we take that first intrepid step forward in a new direction—to take responsibility for our own happiness and learn to bring others joy—we begin to achieve real peace, for ourselves and the world.

Lastly, a note on editing and style before we proceed to the rest of the book: In almost every teaching, Rinpoche discusses several topics which tend to cross over and run in a loop. In keeping the flow of the teachings, we have tried to maintain as much of the essence and structure of the original talks as possible. They have been arranged into separate chapters and sections to highlight specific messages and themes, but, as many of the topics overlap across chapters, they do often make references to each other and are repeated for emphasis.

Original recordings of some of these teachings are also available on CD, DVD or can be viewed online on YouTube.com. These edited transcripts are not meant to replace the talks themselves and it is highly recommended that the reader complement this book by listening to or watching recordings of the talks. It gives a much richer experience and understanding of both the teachings and Rinpoche's dynamic approach to Dharma.

Editor

PUBLISHER'S NOTE

In order to maintain and bring the spirit and passion of H.E. Tsem Rinpoche's teachings to the reader in this compilation, the Publisher has made a conscious decision to preserve the fervor, enthusiasm, colloquial expressions and immediacy of Rinpoche's spoken words, all of which take precedence over syntax and other writing formalities.

The Publisher requests the reader to remember that this book consists of compilations from transcripts of live *viva voce* teachings.

PART I

Peace Begins...

1 PEACE BEGINS...

...With the People You Live With

The real practice right now, for all of us, is to bring incredible harmony to every single person who comes into contact with us.

I want you to be fanatical about yourself: your mind, your relationship with the people you love and with everyone around you. That is what Dharma[1] is about.

Dharma is the love, harmony and the greater understanding that a wife and a husband feel for each other. It is when there are fewer arguments between a wife and a husband, between cousins, between siblings, between children and their parents. It brings people closer together.

Temporarily, Dharma may look like it separates families or takes you away from the people you love but I promise you that in the end Dharma will bring everyone closer together. Nothing in the Buddha's teachings talks about breaking people up. Dharma always encourages us to love other people, to forgive our enemies, to live harmoniously with our partners and to create more peace. It has never, ever taught anything else.

Please do not think that Buddha does not want people to have families and be together with the people we love. Buddha is not trying to turn everyone into monks and nuns! That may have been the predominant method and practice during Buddha's time, about 2,500 years ago, but the situation and times have now changed. Buddha set forth different teachings for different time periods which would better suit the people at that particular moment. The 21st Century is not a time for monasticism and holding vows. To be a monk or a nun, for those who can and want to do so now, is certainly incredible and beautiful, but the main Buddhist teachings at this time are about creating inner and outer peace, because peace is very important to all of us, within and without. Right now, we may not be able to do anything about things happening on the outside, but we can do something about what is within, here and around us.

Today, Dharma is about creating beautiful, harmonious relationships with the people around us, to forgive the wrongs that others have done to us and to forgive ourselves also for the wrongs we have done. Then we move on to becoming happy, light, carefree individuals who can bring this light to other people. We must realize that everything that we have is only for a very, very short time. And the most important thing in our lives are the people who care about us—these are the people who have loyally stayed with us and have been by our side through all our bad habits, bad temper, bad words and anger. It is these people—who have stayed with us over time—who are important. In the end, we might lose everything except these people.

We may have had a lot of bad experiences with some of these people but it does not have to remain this way forever—we can change it. And this change begins with very small steps in whatever you are already doing. It is not something monumental and unachievable! If you have one less argument with your partner, that is Dharma. If you have one less attachment, that is Dharma. If you control your anger once a day, that is Dharma. If you forgive your partner, that is Dharma. That is what Dharma is: it is about bringing people together.

Dharma is about harmony, love, care and forgiveness. The most important thing we must learn to do is to let go. Each one of us has very, very strong attachments that have created some form of disharmony within our families, with our husbands, wives, children, friends or business partners.

The disharmony can arise from only a few things, just as illnesses and diseases arise as a result of only a few causes. Generally, if we know the cause of the illness, we can begin to treat it. In the same way, there are only a few things which can cause disharmony within our families or with the people we love: dishonesty, anger towards our partners and not letting them win an argument, greed or miserliness. It could be because we constantly take advantage of our partners, or make them pay and take care of us, and we don't even know it.

We need to really look back at our lives and ask ourselves what is left for us: just death and perhaps a few people around us who will support us, love us and take care of us. What we need to do now is to start doing what we found difficult to do with our partners and friends before.

For example, if you have been having arguments with your wife, you should stop thinking, "Why is my wife like that?" and start to think instead, "Why do I react to my wife like that?" and let go and change yourself. After all, your wife is not going to be a Buddha overnight.

For now, it would be unhelpful for us to talk about world peace, karma,[2] Enlightenment, future lives, etc. Instead, we should just talk about right now, and how much harmony we can bring into our lives and our families. If we are going to pray for and benefit the world, we should begin with the people we live with. We should treasure the people who we are with—I have given you the example of a wife or husband but you can apply that same teaching to children; children should apply that teaching to their parents and siblings.

Stop sitting there bellyaching and complaining about what you do not have. You may never have it for the rest of your life, so do you want to spend the rest of your life complaining about not having it? Or learn to accept it and make others around you happy? We should stop complaining about our partners, friends, children and life. We should stop sitting there, waiting to cash in on a huge fortune and then move on with life. We might never get what we want for the rest of our lives but we need to keep what we already have now.

Stop looking for money, stop looking for the windfall, stop looking for the other person to change, stop looking for outer transformation—look inside and transform immediately. Change yourself, not them. By accepting who they are, it is transformation. Sometimes we may be surprised by what we get back—when we change, they also change, without us even expecting it.

Gifts do not necessarily have to be material. Sometimes, living peacefully with our partners, friends and family, and not screaming and fighting is a gift in itself. If we can pass one day and one week without fighting and shouting, and without disharmony, that is a big gift. We must not wait for the other person to start. *We* have to start. And please do not think that it ends once you have bought a bouquet of flowers for your spouse and done your part. Your effort to bring harmony to your family has to be continuous.

You know what you are inside. You know your good points—which are many—and you know your few flaws. Start Dharma practice today by transforming your few flaws. It is to stop being cold, calculative and angry, and to stop holding on to the past. It is to begin to forgive, to let go of envy and expectations, and to stop blaming and pointing fingers at others.

I am not asking you to chant more, or recite more prayers and mantras[3]; I am asking you to practice real life Dharma. The real practice right now, for all of us, is to bring incredible harmony and love into our families and to every single person who comes into contact with us. Start there.

Our ability and motivation to create harmony does not come from some mystical sign, like Buddha appearing to us in a dream. The motivation comes from knowing that life is very short and we have already made a lot of mistakes. It comes from an awareness of our own shortcomings and knowing that if we let them continue, they will only become stronger and bigger. However, when we face and overcome those shortcomings, and when we are nice to people regardless of whether they are nice to us—that is Dharma.

2 PEACE BEGINS...

...Even Though Everyone Around You Is a Nightmare

Spiritual practice is about being nice and patient to people who are not nice to you.

I am sure many of you have nightmare husbands or wives, nightmare children, nightmare partners and friends—in fact, everyone around you is a nightmare! I am sure many of you would like to go into a retreat for a while, where you can be alone, far away from everyone else; or send your nightmare friends and partners into retreat!

Let's fantasize for a moment. Start by thinking about someone who really bothers you. Let's say we advise them to go for a retreat[1] for three years, three months and three days[2] and make up a story about how they will become enlightened by this retreat. If they do not believe in Buddha or Enlightenment, we could tell them that the retreat is for luck and that they will attract a great deal of wealth into their lives by this retreat.

All of us then go up to the Himalayas, find an uninhabited mountain and dig out a cave. We fix it up nicely for their "retreat"—make a little built-in toilet, fix up the cave with curtains and heating, install a water supply, pull wiring from Kathmandu up to the Himalayas, install a generator and make sure they stay up there nice and warm. We even put in a CCTV connection there so they can see what we are doing back at home. Then, we lock them in from the outside as they do in Tibetan-style retreats. We are the only ones who have the key and there are no locksmiths in the Himalayas!

Visualize: The helicopter pad is upstairs, and we are all getting in. We are now all inside the helicopter with that one person we would like to send for retreat and we are about to take off. It is a 16-hour ride to the Himalayan mountains but we are happy to do it—for Dharma, we will put up with anything.

We land on top of Mount Everest and we climb out of the helicopter. We open the little door and show them their new apartment in the Himalayas. We are so excited we almost faint! We put them inside the apartment and now, we are turning the key to lock them in. We run back to the helicopter, we climb in and we fly back to Kuala Lumpur.

And now, they are gone.

Those monster partners and friends are in retreat. We do not have to hear their voices again, we do not have to listen to them rant and complain, we do not have to put up with their hang-ups, their weird quirks, their likes and dislikes, and their attachments. We come back home, all by ourselves—no more nagging, no more arguments, no more weird conversations or ideas. Nothing. Wouldn't that be great?

Think about it. What would be easier? Creating this whole scenario or transforming ourselves and learning to look differently at the situation around us? The things that bother us about that person *are real*. But wouldn't it be easier if we just changed ourselves? There are things that bother us about that person, but there will be something else, or something similar, that will bother us about another person. There are only a few things that we can be disturbed by. It would be one thing or another, a combination or a different manifestation of the same thing. It would therefore be easier to transform ourselves first.

When we are trying to engage in spiritual practice, we should actively look for difficult people—they are the best way for us to learn how to transform our minds from negative ways of thinking to open, positive ways of thinking that can embrace difficulties and benefit the other person.

Personally, I want to meet all the people who do not like established religions. I like the people who say they don't want to meditate, who are lazy and greedy. I want to meet the druggies, the prostitutes, the people who are transgendered and the people who have alternative lifestyles. I want to meet all the people who society labels as strange, weird and different. There is a bigger group of those people out there. I do not want to just meet and talk to the holier-than-thou, saintly, good-as-gold people.

The people who I would like to reach out to are people who are just like you and me, who would not normally engage in spiritual practice, who are not interested, who are lazy, who have a lot of weird ideas, who would rather hang out doing nothing or who are preoccupied with other things—those are the people who make up the majority of the planet. Even when we look at people who are already within established religions, how many of them are really practicing what their religions teach? The ones who really practice make up only a very small group.

Many religions cater to these "good" people because it is "easy." It is easy to be nice to someone who is nice to you. They are nice to you, so you are also nice to them. That is not religion; that is not spirituality; that is not Catholicism; that is not Jesus; that is not Buddha; that is not God. It is easy to be nice to someone who is nice to you, but it is not easy to be nice to someone who is *not* nice to you. Religion and spiritual practice is about being nice and patient to people who are *not nice to you*. This is how we bring spirituality to others.

3 PEACE BEGINS...

...Inside "Boobali" and Respecting Female Energy

All women are *dakinis* and they hold up half the sky.

All women are *dakinis*[1] and we should accord them the respect as such. In Buddhism, women are considered the pillars of the family. They provide emotional strength, they are gentle and feminine, yet strong; they are miracle workers. Their energy is wisdom. They produce children and they give their male companions what they want. They give us company and they support us. In Asian societies especially, women are incredible because they are taught to put up with a lot of things from men and they do put up with these things. Women are treasures and we have to respect them as treasures.

Traditionally, what men want is not to come home to a nagging wife who rants and raves, and complains about everything. Men feel that they have worked all day and they just want to come home and have their wives make a nice home for them. Men want their women to be nice little wives, to stay home, to always give them respect and not to cause them any embarrassment. Men like to sit there, be served and be given things. It does not matter if it is wrong or right. In every old culture, tradition has dictated that women serve men.

It is up to you if you wish to follow tradition or if you want to follow logic; that is not really my business. I am not here to change 20,000 years of society and culture. But what I am trying to say is that however we are served by others, we will have to serve others one day. The karma will come back. Everyone wants something from each other. That's natural, isn't it? So why don't we give that to each other? It is something very small.

So take care of your wives—they are *dakinis*, they gave you your children, they give you a lot of pleasure, they gave you company, they have stayed through thick and thin with you. Give back. Imagine yourself running around for nine months with a huge belly! Buddha recognized the value of female energy and made the female Buddhas Vajrayogini[2] and Tara[3] most supreme in the hierarchy of the practices. It is not because women are better than men but—as even Mao Tse Tung recognized—women hold up half the sky.

We need to stop sitting there expecting women to do things for us, we need to reward them. Tomorrow or the day after, immediately, go and buy some flowers for your wife. Yes, it is a little embarrassing and you feel a little stupid but it does not matter. The stupidity and the embarrassment are over really quickly. You have money for your drinks and friends but you do not have money for your wives? That isn't good.

46

Don't be embarrassed. I know that for some of you, after being married for twenty years, you've never even given one *petal* to your wife. So now that you give her flowers, she might wonder what your motive is! It's definitely not *boobali*![4] Some of you haven't had *boobali* with your wives in over fifteen years! I asked some of you when was the last time you had *boobali*, and you couldn't remember!

But it's not really about *boobali*; it's about inside *boobali*. It is the feeling you get from *boobali*—the warmth, the forgiveness and the care—because time is short. So take care of your wives, bring them flowers once every two or three months. Take them out, with no motive. Don't just take them out to the market or to a cheap café and say, "I took you out, so keep quiet now!" Isn't your wife worth a few hundred dollars for a night out?

What are you saving your money for? What are you keeping it for? Even Tutankhamun couldn't take any of the pyramids and all the wealth inside them with him. It's in the British museum now. What do you think you're going to take with you to your next life when you die? Your 100,000 or 200,000 dollars? Remember, you came into this life naked, just holding on to the placenta.

And women, what can you do for men? You know what they want. Men only want one thing. *Just one thing*—to stop being nagged! So just shut up! Don't nag them. You know how men are not expressive, they don't like to talk about things, they don't want to tell you things. So stop nagging your husbands, ranting, complaining and making noise.

I am not just talking about doing that to husbands; I am also talking about your friends, your mother, your aunt or whoever you nag the life out of. Stop. What's the big deal? It's a small price to pay, a very small gift to give back. You get flowers, they don't get nagging—then you get a little bit closer.

And children must serve their parents. You must do this if you want to practice Buddhism, go into retreat, do your *sadhanas*[5] and accomplish things that are of value. Take a look at the children who serve their parents and those who don't serve their parents, and see where they are in life, where their mental level is and how good their minds are.

Even if they cannot serve their parents physically, children who serve their parents mentally—by not fighting back or helping in whatever way they can—usually have a mental attitude that is more pliable, nicer and kinder. They have achieved more in life. The kids who don't get anywhere in life are the ones who don't serve their parents. There's nothing magical here—they show you the nature of their mind and how deep their selfish mind is.

No one in your life, directly or indirectly, has been kinder to you on a physical level than your parents. No one. (This could also be an aunt or uncle who has taken care of you or anyone who has been kind to you—it does not have to be your biological parents.) If you don't take care of and serve your parents, why do you have them? You're doing your *sadhanas* and prayer retreats, and making offerings but you are not holy in any way and you will not gain any attainments if you do not serve your parents. To serve one's parents is a measuring stick of how intense our selfish mind is or not, and of our attainments.

So if you can, serve your parents intensely. If they don't need you physically or if they don't need your service, then serve them mentally. If they don't need your service mentally, then at least don't be a burden to them in any way, now or in the future. That is service to your parents. If we are a burden for them in the past, the present and the future, we are extremely selfish people and we will not get anywhere in our Dharma practice. We will never get anywhere even in life because how we treat our parents reflects our attitude.

Stop looking at your parents' few flaws or thinking that your expectations were not fulfilled. That is a result of your own karma. Holding on to that, and saying that you are not nice to your parents because they didn't do this or that for you is actually a cover-up for your own very selfish mind.

Serve your parents, drive them around, eat with them, call them, take care of them, listen when they talk to you, listen to them with a smile when they tell you the same story 5,000 times and happily ask them what happened, again and again and again. Give them massages and make time for them. Do you know why? Because that's all that's left.

If you don't serve your parents in a physical, mental way, you are not a Dharma practitioner. If you do any higher practices, such as Vajrayogini or Heruka,[6] you will gain zero attainments and zero progress. In fact, you will go backwards. You might do the practice for years but nothing will happen. If you are asking why you are still the same, it is because you do not serve your parents and because the measuring stick of the selfishness of the mind has not lessened. And if your selfishness has not lessened, how can you progress in your *sadhanas*? That is why we do the preliminary practices, which transform the mind to make it pliable and ready for tantric practice. Don't think you just do tantric practice and your life changes.

If you want to do Tantra, you need to take care of your parents, the people who have been kind to you and the people around you—your wives and your husbands. You need to be kind. Don't expect people to serve you; *you* serve them and help them. Don't wait for people to give you things; *you* do it.

Every time someone gives you a cup of tea, and you expect it, you collect the karma and you re-habituate the selfish mind. You harm yourself. You get the moment's thrill but ultimately, it is not good. Don't sit there and wait for money from someone. If you really need it and you get it, it's wonderful; but don't blackmail and manipulate for it.

The message here is that it's time to bring Dharma home. I want everyone to make an effort. If you think of me as your Lama,[7] spiritual guide or teacher, that is my instruction to you. If you think of me as a friend, that is my request. If you think of me as a nice person who has lived life and who knows a little bit more, this is me on my knees begging and pleading with you. It doesn't matter to me how you wish to view me. But you need to do that. You need to lessen the mind that brings harm to yourself.

I'm talking about family values, and welding families and people together, because peace and love come from that. Even when we do ceremonies for monks and nuns here in the future, it is not about taking people away from their families; it is about letting them live in austerity for a while to realize how much they have.

I want your *sadhanas* not to be another mantra or another initiation, running after another Lama. How many living Buddhas have you been sitting in front of and getting initiations from? And look at you, you're worse! You're not a living Buddha, you're a living nightmare! You don't need any more initiations and practices and all that. What you need is to take your mother and father out for dinner once a week, to take your wife or husband out for dinner once a week, to not nag your husband. Listen when people tell you what is wrong with you and then stop being that way.

You want to do a *sadhana* every week? That is it. Do something for the very people that you live with, immediately, because that is Dharma, that is your *sadhana*. I'm not telling you to go home and chant mantras. Do you want to be spiritual? Buy flowers for your wife and take her out for a meal. Stop nagging your husband. Don't cheat on your husbands and wives, in any way. You want the greatest *Yidam*?[8] The greatest *Yidam* is getting behind a steering wheel and taking your mother or father out to eat. You want the greatest mantra? The greatest mantra is, "How are you Mummy? How are you Daddy? What can I do for you?" That is the greatest mantra, at this moment, for us.

Do you know what's the greatest mind? The greatest mind is not wanting other people to change, but you yourself changing and accepting other people. The greatest mind is to stop wondering when they will change. No. You should think instead, "When will *I* change?" That is the greatest practice.

So, if you believe in God, that's fabulous; if you believe in Buddha, that's fabulous; if you don't believe in anything, that's fabulous. But please believe in yourself and please believe in the happiness you can bring to people around you. Believe in that. Wouldn't that be lovely?

4 PEACE BEGINS...

...When We Live for Others

When we have the attitude that our practice is for others, we will never give up.

The secret of Dharma is not to expect everyone around you to be fabulous and enlightened. No, that is not Dharma. Dharma is your ability not to become discouraged, no matter what others do to you. This is because your motivation is never based *on* them; your motivation is *for* them. When we are in Dharma, proper motivation is essential from Day One.

If our motivation is based on others, then of course our moods will go up and down. If our motivation is *for* others, then whether they are up or down, our mood will always be up and we will also want to make the mood of others to go up.

"If they practice, then I will practice" is a common excuse given by people whose motivation is based on others. On the other hand, people whose motivation is for others will say,

"For the sake of others, I will study the Dharma. For the sake of others, I will listen to and read the Dharma. For the sake of others, I will meditate and pray, and I will put up with difficulties." When our motivation is for the sake of others, we will not become depressed or angry, and we will not give up.

Let me give you an example. If we love someone very much—such as our children or our siblings—would we ever give up on them, no matter what they do to us? They might take all our money and ruin our reputation but we would never give up on them.

We are able to do this because we are doing it *for* them. We want them to be happy and to have a good life; we want them to have realizations. Even if it takes up to 30 years for them to gain one realization, even if we are on our death bed and we see that they still have not gained any realizations, we would advise them, on our last breath, to take care of themselves. We would tell them things like, "Don't let that person cheat you" or "Don't go with that nasty girl." Even on our last breath, we would say something for their benefit.

Some dying mothers still find the energy to say to their children, "Don't lose the crops...don't forget to water the crops!" just before they die! Why is this? It is because they have never lived on the basis of their children doing anything for them but they have lived for their children. When we live for others, our attitude will be different.

There are people who get upset easily or make a lot of excuses when they join a Dharma center. Some of them say they do not want to practice because everyone in the group is already a saint and the practices are too high a standard for them! I have heard people say things like, "I quit the group because they are all too wonderful" or "They're too advanced for me so I'm getting out of here!" How silly! You are not doing it for them! On the other hand, I have also heard people say, "Nobody here practices, I'm getting out of here!"

Either way, both types of people have the wrong motive. When you make excuses like that, you are practicing on the basis of others, instead of practicing for them. Even if they *are* enlightened, there are another five billion people out there who are not! If they are not enlightened, join the other five billion people out there who are not! Therefore, our practice should not be based on other people or on the group that we have joined. It should be based on compassion for them, for others.

Our spiritual practice cannot be on the basis of how others treat us. Our spiritual practice also cannot be conditional and on the basis of "*if* I have this, *if* I have that, *if* I get this, *if* that person is like that, *if* the group is like that," etc. How are we going to gain attainments if our mind keeps going up and down based on these conditions? Some people just drop out of spiritual practice and disappear from their centers whenever little things happen. Why? Their practice was not for anyone, not even for themselves! It was on the basis of other people. They practiced because it allowed them to get together socially; because it was an opportunity for fun or for intellectual stimulation.

Compare that to people who practice for others—they will have a different attitude. They can go through tremendous hardship and severe beatings and not be disheartened or give up the Dharma. You can read the histories of many people who, because of their faith, were tortured, shocked with electric prods, raped and emasculated. They had their limbs cut off, they were beaten and burned to force them to give up their beliefs but they would not. They would not give up their practice because they did not practice on the basis of whether they were in a comfortable situation and free from harm. Because they practiced for others, they were able to bear the suffering. This can be seen across all religions, which have all experienced persecution at one time or another in history.

Therefore, it is important for us to set a proper motivation from the very first day we step into Dharma and to remember that we should do Dharma *for others*. When you do Dharma for others, you will not make excuses or say things like, "This person did that to me so I'm not going to the center anymore. That person said that to me and that is why I'm not doing anything at the center anymore. They're not organized, they're not ready, they don't have money, they don't have a system, they're mean, they're rude."

Yes! We all complain about things like that! Welcome to *samsara*![1] Are we going to say that we won't practice because of all those things? It's so silly! It is silly to think that way because we are not going to find perfect practice anywhere. However, if we change our attitude, everything becomes perfect, because everything that we encounter then becomes practice.

This is why Dharma practitioners who really want to make a difference in the lives of others will thrive on confusion, anger and mischief. They will thrive on nasty, weird people and people who totally test their patience. They will thrive on all those emotions and those types of people because they are not disturbed by them. They think of all the difficulties they encounter as opportunities to practice the Dharma by absorbing those difficulties and transforming their minds.

When we have this change of attitude and we begin to practice for others, we will not be disappointed and we will not be sad. We will be able to bear all difficulties, whatever is said or done to us, and whatever happens around us; even if we have to lose people or give up on people, we will never give up on our practice.

Lord Buddha lost his parents, his wife, Yasodhara, and his beautiful son, Rahula. In ancient Indian tradition, the first-born son is very precious and highly regarded; for him to lose his son and his wife would have been unbearable if he had not had the motivation of gaining Enlightenment for others. He had prestige, power, money, youth, a beautiful body, fabulous hair, great clothes, the elephants, the armies and all that he stood to inherit from his father!

Nowadays, when we know our parents are rich, many of us sit around waiting for the wealth to come to us. The minute one of our parents passes away, our attitude becomes incredibly blasé—we hurry through the traditional mourning rituals, we mumble a few mantras, "*Om Mani Peme Hung*,[2] see you later, hope you take a great rebirth, let's dedicate a Buddha statue to you. See you later Mummy, see you later Daddy. Can I have the money now?!"

After we get the money, we pay off our bills, pay for who or what we want, take our girlfriend or boyfriend and fly away to wherever we have been dying to go. We think to ourselves,

"Thank God somebody died so I would *not* die waiting to go on holiday!"

On a daily basis, we probably do not think in such a negative way but subconsciously, that type of thinking is definitely there because we have been thinking that way for many lifetimes. This type of thinking reflects that we are dependent on other people and do not take responsibility. Thinking like that about our parents' wealth is natural. It is not evil but it is natural—all of us have, in one way or another, sponged off our parents at some point. All of us.

Therefore, we should repay the kindness of our parents in this life, past lives and future lives. We can do this by changing our attitude and by doing things for others. By doing things for others, we collect great amounts of merit,[3] which we can then dedicate to all other sentient beings, including our very kind parents. We do not collect any further negative karma and in that way, we can repay their kindness.

Every time we are aware, we repay their kindness. Every time we stop our anger and we reduce it, we repay their kindness. In this way, when we practice Dharma, we practice for others and we repay their kindness. When we have the attitude that our practice is for others, we will never give up, just as we do not give up on our parents or children, boyfriends or girlfriends, wives or husbands. We will not give up.

When you do this and think like this, a growing sense of universal responsibility will open up in your mind and that is when your motivation grows to wanting to bring happiness to everyone who comes to you. You start to think that whatever method you have to employ or whatever you have to sacrifice, you will do it for others because others are more important than you alone.

It is my passion to bring Dharma to others. This means that for even one person, I will bear anything—for example, I am willing to be sick or give them whatever they want. I am able to bear this because if that one person can then convey the Dharma to other people, my passion will have been fulfilled.

The purpose of our center has always been, is and always will be, to help people gain knowledge to change their perspective, regardless of whether they are Buddhist or not. We want to help them to change their perspective because their suffering will then become less.

My encouragement for the many departments of Kechara in Malaysia and Nepal—such as the publishing house, the soup kitchen, the outlets and the arts department—is because all departments are extensions of my passion to bring Dharma to others, in any way, shape or form. I also feel passionate when talking to people who share that passion. It is not just because we share the same dream; I also admire that they have compassion. I can draw inspiration from this compassion. I know that we do Dharma work, strive very hard, do not give up and really pursue our Dharma work because we have compassion for others. Compassion begets compassion. It is very simple.

5 PEACE BEGINS...

...Before Your Husband Dies

We need to bring more harmony, love, care and forgiveness into our families, *immediately*, because they can be gone at any time.

What we need to do now is real Dharma practice, and real practice is controlling ourselves and forgiving the pain that we've experienced. Forgiving the pain we experience does not mean we let it happen again but the method we employ not to let it happen again must be Dharma.

It must be Dharma because we do not want to collect any more negative karma. If people want to hurt us, cheat us and do things that damage us, they are going to get their karma back. (However, this does not mean that you sit there and count the days when they are going to get their karma back because then you are just as bad as them.)

You don't let them hurt you but you also cannot hurt them back and you cannot be negative back towards them. It is very, very simple: whatever negativity you wish upon them and however much you punish them is how much karma you will get back in the future. You must have had some karma to even meet these people and to be around them in the first place.

We need to bring more harmony, love, care and forgiveness into our families—immediately. Not tomorrow. Not next week. *Immediately*, because they can be gone at any time. You know how fragile life is.

I was reading an article in an old copy of *Readers' Digest* about all the people who died in the tsunami in 2004; the article had emotional pictures of people holding their children or wives who had died. You can see the shock of the moment in those pictures. I saw a photo of a father standing over his dead son—the emotion that he showed and of the people watching him was incredible. It becomes instilled in you and you feel the loss. It is a loss that is irreplaceable.

Any of us can feel that. I felt scared and moved because I knew I could be in that position—I could lose people I care about. Wives, husbands and children can go anytime—they may not even die, but just go. Do we want that?

Before that happens—and it is going to happen—we need to do something now. That's what Dharma is about. It's not about who's right and who's wrong, whose Dharma center is big, which religion is right, whether there's a future life or not, whether Buddha exists or God exists, whether Catholicism is the real religion or Buddhism is the real religion. It's not about any of that. It's about us bringing harmony into our families, into our lives, into the people we care about NOW. That's what it's about. And that's why we learn Dharma.

I want you to have another perspective. Right now, you find out that your husband or your wife has died. No more. You go home and your partner, your friend, your mother, your daughter, your sister, your wife or your husband is dead. You go home alone and there's 49 days of mourning to prepare for...

Think about all that because you know what? It's going to happen one day. You're going to go home and receive news that your partner has died. Your aunt is dead. Your father is dead. Your wife is dead. Your husband is dead. Your mother will never breathe again and you will never see her again. Now how do you feel? Now who wins? What about the last argument? The last nagging session? The last fight? The last time you sat there in anger and thought, "They did this and they did that to me"? Think about that.

You know what's the fear behind all that? *It will happen.* None of us can escape that. I'm not talking about Buddha and heaven and hell and all that; I'm not trying to scare you with a lot of theology. I'm telling you a basic human fact— you will hear that someone has died. All of you. You don't need psychic powers for that.

I'm giving you stark reality. Some of you say that you have a nice husband, he supports you and takes care of you financially. That's beautiful and there's nothing wrong with that but what happens when you find out he's dead and there's no more financial support? What about all the rubbish and difficulties that you created for that person while he was alive?

And you know what's the horrible part? You live on and you could probably find a new husband but the habituation of creating problems for others would still be very strong in you and you'll continue to create problems for the next person. But will they take it?

Then what happens? What do you do then? Work on yourselves now, today, immediately. What is of value, after all, to you? For some of us, it's our Dharma practice and our future lives; for some of us, it's happiness; for some of us, it's money; for some of us, it's company. We all have different value systems but we do value something and I'm sure we all value the people that we're with. That's the bottom line.

Listen to what your partners, friends and family are saying and give them what they want. Listen to what they nag about and give to them. Regardless of their nagging, give to them. In giving to them, you give to yourselves—in the most worldly sense, they stop nagging! In giving to yourselves, you give to others, because the happier you become, the more you can do for others. And the only way to create happiness for yourself is by making other people happy.

PART II

Peace Comes...

...With Real Giving

Being consistent is a form of giving that is extremely beneficial; it is a very, very big part of giving.

When we think about the people we cherish the most—such as friends, uncles, aunts, brothers and sisters, our dear mothers and wonderful fathers—we treasure them tremendously and they are the most beautiful people in the world to us. But treasuring them tremendously does not automatically equate to them having superior wisdom. They may have intelligence, knowledge and worldly, street-wise know-how but that does not equate to wisdom. Our love for someone and their kindness to us does not equate to them having superior wisdom or the wisdom of a Buddha.

So we do things out of love for them that could be wrong. It may be good immediately but it could be damaging to them in the long term. What we should do is to skillfully learn the

Dharma and bring Dharma to them through our actions, not merely through our explanations.

Sometimes, when we have been in Dharma for a few years, we start trying to explain things to people who are older, more educated and experienced. They may feel like we are treating them like a child because they are used to seeing us in a child-like position. So, even if we gain more wisdom and we start talking to them, it may not be beneficial immediately. However, we can bring Dharma to our friends, our children, people we love and people who have been very kind to us by acting in accordance with the Dharma.

You may wonder how you can practice deep and profound Dharma at this level, immediately. To act in accordance with the Dharma is very, very simple. Deep and profound Dharma is not Tantras or deities, wearing ornaments of the gods or pendants, giving away millions of dollars and gifts. Giving is not a big deal. When you look at the world, a lot of movie stars made it big because they "gave" something and they got something back. If you are a beautiful woman in a big, cosmopolitan city, for example, you will probably make it. You have given something so that they will give you something back. That is not real giving. That is actually based on self-grasping.

Giving is not based on one's wealth. Never use your financial position as a basis for giving, or whether you can or cannot give. If you equate that with giving, you are absolutely, one hundred percent wrong. There are many, many ways to give that are far more superior than giving just money (but we should not use that as an excuse for being miserly and stingy either, or because we simply do not wish to give. We must not let our mind games win).

Real giving is very, very different. Real giving is not determined by the people who give or who receive, or how or where the giving is done. Real giving cannot be judged. Real giving cannot be fathomed. Real giving has benefits for the giver and the recipient, and the benefits are not short-term; they are long-term and extend into many future lives. If it is totally correct from the beginning, that action of giving returns and never stops until you become a fully enlightened Buddha.

A mother giving her child an education in school is not really giving, although I know that's a little shocking for all of you to hear. It is a form of giving but it is not real giving. It is an attachment, where the mother thinks, "Me, me, me, mine, mine, mine, my child, I want." If you really care about people, why do you select your own child? I'm not trying to break values, to tell you to stop educating your children. I'm giving you the truth. You should continue to give to and take care of your loved ones but do not equate that completely with real giving.

There are many, many levels to giving; on an outer level and an inner level. Being consistent is a form of giving that is extremely beneficial; it is a very, very big part of giving. Consistency is when you say you are going to do something and you do it, you continue to do it and you see it through to the end. You benefit the people around you and the people you love. Saying that you are going to take on a project and finish it—and you do it—is giving.

If you volunteer for certain activities in the Dharma center, you do them, finish them, continue to do them and don't do them just to please people, then that is giving. This is a kind of giving where you give people confidence about you. You give yourself confidence. You re-habituate yourself to be something different. Giving is very, very profound.

If you give consistently—whether it is to sweep your house for your partner or to sweep the Dharma center—and you do it without being chased, watched and told, that is giving. You are giving so much because when someone depends on you and you give to them, it helps other people who depend on them, and the other people who depend on them, etc. You are giving and it spreads.

For example, I might promise a friend that I will give him a lift to work every Tuesday. I should do it every week and not make any lame excuses; if for any reason I cannot give him a lift, I should make other arrangements and inform him. You see, he may have made other arrangements—such as letting his parents use his car that day; or not asking his other friends to give him a lift; or saving some money from petrol so that he can put his savings towards a new Buddha statue. It affects a lot of people.

Actually, we are already being consistent all the time. We assess ourselves every day. If we are movie stars or fashion models, we assess our physical appearance. If we are real estate agents, we assess ourselves and our knowledge of the area. If we are kings or queens, we assess ourselves constantly based on what the public thinks about us—whether we're dressed right, what we should do, what our etiquette should be.

We are already doing that all the time. Don't think of that as anything different from the Dharma; don't make Dharma different from your normal life. Dharma is not different from your normal life. Dharma is life.

When we give, it doesn't have to be money. It can be a very deep type of giving—inner giving. Giving is consistency. Love comes from consistency. Consistency is if you say you are going to do it, you do it. We all have bad days and ugly days but we can't use that over and over again to be in a bad mood, to be unreliable, nasty, ugly, mean and rude, and spread that to others. They may always forgive us but can we forgive ourselves? And when we forgive ourselves, will people still be around?

Don't tell me you don't have money. You couldn't have reached this stage of your life if you didn't. Don't tell me that when you get a million dollars, you will do this and that. If it isn't going to happen, it isn't going to happen. If you don't have the right attitude now, you won't have it later when the money comes either. And even if the money does come, you are going to have plenty of other things to do with it.

Don't say that you don't have the financial means or material capability to be consistent, to love the people around you and to show them that you love them. There are many people who don't have material support but are very happy with others around them.

To be consistent with whatever you do and to break away from the negative habits that you have is very, very, very important. If you have a Dharma motivation and you think, "I want to make the center grow, I'm going to be consistently kind, I'm not going to raise my voice, I'm going to clean, I'm going to sweep, I'm going to make offerings, I'm not going to complain," and you make a commitment to the Buddhas, to your teacher, to yourself and you do it consistently, that is Dharma practice.

If you want to please the Buddhas, your Lamas, your Dharma brothers and sisters, and if you want to die with confidence, you need to practice consistency. That is new-age. That is Buddhism. That is life. That is true. That appeals to everyone, all over. If you want to view it from a Buddhist's perspective of consistency, then you are a Buddhist practitioner. If you want to do it from the standpoint of your love for someone, that is true love. If you want to do it as a means of self-improvement, it is real self-improvement.

Giving starts this moment, with your mind breaking its habituations. Having these habituations is not evil. None of us are evil. It is the cultural programming which we have received throughout our lives. From very strong cultures (such as the Chinese, European and American cultures) where money, family, education and status, etc., are highly valued, we can turn these things around to be used for even bigger things. The attitude is there. It is how we use this attitude for bigger things to benefit ourselves and others.

So Dharma practice starts now. Don't take on 20 commitments. Just take on two or three. And don't swear to the whole planet, to all sentient beings that we are going to do this. We are not Kuan Yin.[1] Let's accept that. What I accept instead is, "I am Tsem Rinpoche and I have limited mental capabilities and limited consistency, but I will make it grow."

The goal of life is to be happy. Don't even talk about Enlightenment yet because you will have excuses about that too! You say, "I don't have to worry about that. That's too far away. Don't worry about me." That's fine, I agree with you at this moment. But what about your parents, your loved ones, your husband, your wife, your children and your friends? What about you loving them and showing it? You can do this by being consistent.

So if you make a promise to your parents, do it! Do it at all costs—at the cost of yourself, your interaction with friends, your own pleasures and your time. Do it! If it is a promise to your daughter or your son, do it. If it is a promise to your clients and friends, do it. If it is a superior promise to a Dharma center, do it. And do it consistently. Being consistent is extremely important. Being consistent to our loved ones is very important. When we develop that, it extends to other people.

On a higher level, we may feel helpless about helping other beings, knowing that we cannot do anything directly for them now. But we can start by being consistent and keeping our promises at the cost of our lives. I don't mean to be that dramatic but that's how much effort we should put into our practice. We should be consistent with whatever we are doing to help people and with whatever promises we have made.

I will give you a very superior *Yidam*, an excellent "secret tantric" practice: Never make people chase you. Never let people remind you. That is the highest tantric deity practice. That is better than Tsongkhapa's,[2] Vajrayogini's or

Dzambala's[3] practices. Never let people chase you in any way, shape or form.

Don't wait for someone to remind you. Let's not even talk about the pain you have created for another mind; the minute you let someone remind you, you let yourself lose because you re-habituate that negativity and the negative attitude in you becomes stronger. Why would you want to do that? It only creates more unhappiness.

How long do you think the people you love can last with you and the way you talk? They may love you but they may not want to be with you. They may care about you but they may not be able to live with you or stand you. They may help you for the rest of your life and always be there for you but they cannot physically be with you because you create a lot of pain for yourself and it hurts them.

You will attract your own kind. Look around you: at the friends you have, at the people around you and their level, and you will know what you are attracting. If you are around people who cheat you, that is what you are attracting and that is the energy you are sending out. If you are consistently around people who are moody and down, and who don't want to do or accomplish anything, you need to think if maybe that is you and if that is what you are attracting.

If we are attracting that negative energy—sour faces, scolding, people ignoring us—we have to think, "Yes, I am getting that, they are doing that to me but am I doing that too?" Don't just sit there justifying and explaining back and forth. Do something about it.

7 PEACE COMES...

... By Looking Beyond the Altar of Ourselves

When you have awareness, you make people around you suffer less.

Consistency arises from awareness, which is the root to all patterns of behavior. Awareness is a very powerful human practice, a human tool that will make us happy, harmonious, loving, caring and alert. Awareness creates awareness. "Awareness" practice, alertness and consistency brings awareness. We begin to know the needs of others.

That is why the practices and monks in the holy traditions of the southern forms of Buddhism such as in Burma, Cambodia, Laos, Sri Lanka and Thailand all focus strictly on *Vipassana*.[1] I have seen it in Bodhgaya. They walk up and down the temple with their eyes closed or semi-closed, with one foot in front of the other, slowly focusing on the breath. They block out everything but in blocking out, everything gets absorbed because their minds become focused. They practice that for years. I've read about great Burmese masters and Thai masters in the north that do this practice of awareness and gain exalted states.

It is not to torture them. It is to bring awareness to their mind, so that their minds do not get distracted by other activities at that time. With the practice of awareness, the first thing is that their immediate harm to others—knocking things down, breaking things, forgetting appointments, promises and commitments, and not caring—is lessened and is eventually cut off.

On the next level, they are able to absorb knowledge very fast because their minds are focused. The knowledge is put into use and they do not need people to police them anymore.

Then, they go to a higher form of practice of awareness where they practice awareness well and deeply (this does not mean that it takes years; it means they put in concentrated effort). They start remembering and recalling things early in their childhood that were stored in their minds; they will even start recalling things in their mother's womb. If we can do it through regression therapy, we can definitely do it in meditation because regression therapy is not something new. When it gets even higher, and more subtle, they will start seeing different types of lights at different stages; their concentration becomes very deep.

Awareness meditation has nothing to do with you blacking and blanking everything out and just sitting there knowing nothing. In the initial stages of awareness meditation, you blank things out, not for the sake of blanking them out but for the sake of focusing on your mind. And what is the mind? Awareness.

When you reach higher states of awareness, your memory becomes clear and you can recall things easily; whatever is absorbed into your mind is not forgotten. You could have met a thousand people and you would not forget them, their habits, what they like and even what food they like to eat. You will not forget.

For example, His Holiness the 14th Dalai Lama has an incredible, incredible ability to remember you even after 10, 20, 30 or 40 years. He remembers what you like, who your deity is, what practice you like and even when he met you. And he meets thousands and thousands of people a year. It is incredible! I know for sure that that is a sign (as it says in the scriptures) that he has achieved *shamatha*—awareness.

It is not magical. If you actually sit, focus and relax, you can remember things much better. If you fluster—there's music, people shouting, your kids screaming, your dogs barking—you cannot concentrate. But if you concentrate and develop this practice of awareness, you will be still inside even if there is chaos and turmoil around you.

There are renowned Thai, Burmese and Cambodian monks and laypeople I've read about who, even in this century, have stayed in awareness meditation for three to six days continuously without moving. I don't want to just keep talking about Tibet because this is not a gift of Tibet; it is a gift of Buddha. All these Thai, Burmese and Cambodian monks may not have to offer silver bowls, brocades and butterlamps on their altars but they are offering much more. Are we doing that?

When you have awareness, you make people around you suffer less. Do you know why? When you are not aware and you need to be told at all times what to do, you burden people around you. You may talk big, use fancy words and explain yourself away. It works the first or second time, but not all the time. It becomes like the little boy who cried wolf.

From a lack of awareness, a lack of consistency arises in our mind. We think that only we are right, our way is right. From that arises anger, which blasts through everything. When we have anger, we cannot see anything or anyone. We only see what we want to. When the anger subsides—whether it takes ten years, ten months or ten days—we will look back at all that we have done out of anger, and there will be nothing but regret, perhaps towards the people we love. The things we cared about will be gone.

Treasuring our anger is equivalent to us saying, "I don't treasure the people I love." And for Dharma practitioners, it is equivalent to saying, "I don't take refuge in the Three Jewels." With anger, the blessings of the Three Jewels cannot enter. With anger, your loved ones cannot be with you. With anger, you destroy yourself. Even if you are 80 years old, you destroy yourself. Whether you want to look at anger from the lower, middle or high points of view, or from a Dharmic point of view, it is destructive. From the human point of view, it is destructive. From the self-improvement point of view, it is destructive.

But if we practice awareness and focus on that, we will see our anger lessen. People whose anger grows with age are like babies in the nurturing stages—their minds move back and forth. It shows that they have done zero practice. There is no Dharma practice and no practice for themselves.

Let's not even talk about Dharma practice yet. We should practice caring for the people who we love. Just practice. What is practice? To improve with every year. If we don't improve, whatever we are holding onto now will be lost very quickly. It will be irrevocably lost. Whatever we put all our energy into on an external level cannot be maintained. We don't create the causes for it to be maintained.

You might have a fabulous boyfriend and you "keep" him by wearing low-cut blouses with short mini skirts and fancy make-up, by ensuring you are always beautiful and your hair is perfect. You know what? There are another 20 million women who look like you, or even better. What's to say your pretty eyes don't look like someone else's?

But if you maintain or love the person with love, compassion, forgiveness and consistency, you have a higher chance of "keeping" him (in most cases). It is the same for our parents and our friends. Through the cultivation of these qualities, you stand a higher chance of keeping them, but it is harder. It seems easier to work on the external—changing our hairstyle or clothes, wearing something sexy or changing jobs, cars and watches. Think about how many times we have done that in our lives. It is much harder to change the inside because the benefits are greater.

So if we are at a certain age, or at a certain point of our life, we need to reflect and ask ourselves, "What did I do wrong? Who have I hurt? Where does that come from? That person is like this or like that but what about me? Was I inconsistent? Was I not aware?"

Make yourself and the people you love happy by asking and telling yourself, "Why do I make myself unhappy? Why do I make other people unhappy? I don't want to." Nobody wakes up, looks at a picture of himself, praises himself and says, "I'm going to make everybody I meet unhappy today."

Actually, we make "offerings" of gold, cloths and silver bowls to statues of ourselves. We "pray" to ourselves by saying, "I'm going to make myself more unhappy." Some of us have been doing that. We don't pray to the Buddha; we pray to ourselves, we take pictures and make statues of ourselves, and we offer gold to ourselves because we are sacred. We think, "Me, me, me, I am sacred; nobody else is."

We make tremendous "offerings" to ourselves: by fighting with others, disappointing others, not being aware, being rough in our speech, showing anger on our faces, not having patience and complaining about others constantly. That is how we make an altar and a shrine to ourselves.

You *should* make an altar and a shrine to yourselves but not that way. How should you do it? By waking up and saying, "I'm going to make myself and others happy. I will continue to do that consistently." Acknowledge that you will fall down sometimes and that you will keep falling down, but know that you can get up. (Don't make that an excuse either. You shouldn't fall and stay down.)

I myself am happy. I'm not one hundred percent happy, and I'm not as happy as the Buddha, but I am happy. And I've realized why. Out of ten bad points I had, I faced up to three or four. I'm still battling them but it is much easier to face up to them now. I am consistently facing them and I'm going to keep doing it. And that's why I'm happier.

Awareness—awareness practice and awareness meditation—is the most powerful practice we can do. Awareness is very powerful. Ask yourself, what is the most powerful motivation for practicing and for keeping awareness with consistency? Do you love the people who are close to you in your life? That's all it is. Do you want to advance in your Dharma practice, or not? Just ask yourself that. If the answer comes out as a "yes," there is a very strong reason to practice awareness. If the answer comes out as a "no," well, in time it will become a "yes." Because truth is truth, truth cannot be changed.

Love the people around you and love them not just by words. Love them by action. Consistency and change will arise through awareness of what you have done and what you are doing.

8 PEACE COMES...

...If We Create Change

When we do spiritual practice, our perspective changes everything around us, and at the same time, nothing changes.

People who feel lazy and unenthusiastic towards spiritual practice usually do not find a lot of meaning in their lives. This is not because their lives do not have meaning but because they do not give their lives meaning.

When we want to give our life meaning, it is not a matter of acquiring external wealth or necessities. It has nothing to do with outer betterment. If giving our life meaning had to do with our outer achievements, and inner betterment at only a very gross level, then we would see drastic changes in our lives once we acquired those material things.

If we examine our lives on a deeper level, we will see that we are usually chasing one thing after another. We are constantly pursuing what we call "goals" and in the process of chasing after goals, we feel happier. However, we have to ask ourselves if that "happiness" is permanent. Usually, once we achieve our first goal, we want another goal. We change our goals—we want a higher goal, a better goal or a different goal.

In the process of chasing goals, we lose time and our youth, and we lose our friends. Sometimes, we lose our partners and those who are close to us. Sometimes, we lose things that really, really matter in our lives. We have to take stock and think: when we chase after these goals, they have to be legitimate and they have to bring about some kind of stable, *unchanging* happiness.

People who are stuck on being happy and stuck on believing they have everything are comfortable just living within their own creations. The key word here is "creation" because it is something these people have created for themselves, it is not real. When something happens to their creation and it disappears or diminishes, their world falls apart.

Similarly, on the opposite end of the spectrum, people who do not want to do anything with their lives, and consistently fail time after time, fail not because of external or internal circumstances. They fail because of their perspective of themselves and the world around them.

Both these perspectives are flawed because they do not bring unchanging happiness to us. Spiritual practice has to do with everything about you changing, and the beauty of it is that nothing changes! Why? As you do more and more spiritual practice—real, transformative spiritual practice— you will see your mind become light, very happy and bright. Spiritual practice is basically a change in attitude. Even if you have only been in spiritual practice for a few months, you will see that you accept things more. Some people start to see their minds expanding after only a few days or weeks.

For example, whatever you would not have normally been able to tolerate, you will be able to tolerate now. You may have thought before that there were some things you would never be able to do or want to do. But sometimes after even one week of being in the Dharma, when people request something of you, you will be able to listen, think about it with your heart and mind, and say, "Yes, I can bear it."

The beautiful part about being engaged in spiritual practice is that there will be a lot more coming! Do you know why? Because you will reach a state where you can take everything, you can perceive everything and you can accept everything. What is the big deal about that transformation? You might think to yourself that you do not want to bear a lot of things! It is not just about bearing things. It is about your attitude.

Why should we change our attitude? When we are cushioned and when things are taken care of for us, life will of course be very easy. However, are we sure that life will always be like that? We might be cushioned physically—for example, our parents have given us a house or our partner has bought us a car—but are we cushioned mentally? Do we remain mentally stable and cushioned throughout our relationships with people, in our finances, jobs and friendships?

If we are not cushioned mentally and we are not prepared, our whole world will fall apart the minute something external changes. For example, the minute someone leaves us or we lose some money, our whole reality will fall apart. The minute someone shows us a sour face and says something unpleasant to us, our reality will fall apart.

When our reality falls apart, we affect everybody around us: the way we act, the way we talk and the way we react in these situations will hurt everybody around us. We can cause a lot of damage to people around us by our reactions. Sometimes, it takes a long time to recover from the damage or, in the worst cases, people never recover from the damage at all.

Therefore, when we do spiritual practice, it changes our minds. It is not that we pray more, meditate more or read more. Spiritual practice changes our minds because it is a change of attitude or perspective, and the way we look at things. Our perspective changes everything around us, and at the same time, nothing changes. Nothing at all.

When we apply the teachings of Buddha, everything about how we perceive and react to people, and how we talk to them; everything about our emotions, delusions, jealousies, successes, motivations and enthusiasms completely changes.

And yet nothing changes. We remain as we are and we retain our identity: male, female, Malaysian, foreigner, we like to eat this type of food, we like going to sleep at this time, we like to wear these kinds of clothes or dress in this type of fashion. None of the external things change but our whole perspective and approach to these things completely changes.

Twenty years ago, we may have dressed to seduce and conquer, and we were great at doing it! We may still dress to impress now, but not for the purposes of conquering or seducing. Perhaps we now dress to impress the people we need to work with or meet, to accomplish something.

We may have dressed up in the past to attract nice girls in a club. Now, we dress up to get a good job in order to support our families. The act of washing, dressing and grooming remains the same and nothing about the whole process has changed. What has changed, however, is the motivation behind why we do it and the objective. Therefore, spiritual practice is the transformation of our perspective, and how we look at and approach things.

The study of the Dharma itself is not Dharma. Praying is not Dharma. Altars and making offerings is not Dharma, whether you hang around a holy Guru or not is not Dharma, having a great Dharma center is not Dharma. Dharma is the complete turnaround of our attitude and the way we perceive the things around us. Everything else is to facilitate that.

As I have always stressed, and as all traditions of Buddhism stress, Buddhist practice is not about offering incense; it is not about having altars or statues, doing prostrations or making water offerings[1]; it is not just doing Dharma work or charity work. Buddhist practice is perspective.

I will give you a clear example. There are people in all religions who know all the rituals, the prayers and how to chant. They attend all the classes and read all the books but when they deal with people, they are exactly the same as they were the first day they embraced their religion—they are still very mean and are not nice at all.

On the other hand, there are also people in every religion whose minds transform as soon as they begin their spiritual practice, from the very first time they hear their minister, pastor, Guru or spiritual guide talk about truth. How can you see that their minds have transformed? They are able to tolerate things that are not bearable and put up with things that they would not have been able to put up with before.

Dharma is not about other people and whether they are practicing Dharma or not. It is not about your neighbors, friends or anyone else; it is about *your* ability to tolerate the situations and people around you. Think about this well—your ability to tolerate people who are not practicing Dharma, who are not doing spiritual practice or who are not good people; your ability to put up with them happily and continuously, is Dharma.

When you reach that stage where you are able to tolerate so much more from others, what you will exude is not negative energy but positive energy. Every single person who comes to you will leave you feeling happy.

Think about how you feel when you go near some people. Some people make us feel stupid; some make us feel very serious. Sometimes, around certain people, we feel confused. Some people make us lose our motivation—we feel very motivated until we speak to them, after which they make us feel uneasy. Those kinds of people bring us down with their energy. Certain people make us feel very angry after being with them for only a short while. We listen to their perspective, how they speak and their views, and it makes us feel uncomfortable.

There are also people who make us feel happier after we have been with them. It is not a happiness which arises from just joking around and having fun but a real happiness, which arises because they have given us something new to think about or a new way of thinking.

How we feel when we leave a person—confused, happy, sad or unhappy—is a state of that person's mind and what their motivation is towards us. If we usually feel happy when we leave a person, it is because that person's mind is focused on bringing happiness to other people.

On our part, wouldn't it be nice if people were happy after having been with us? We can achieve this if we transform our minds and listening to the Dharma can help us to do that. We should think about the effect we would like to leave on the people who come into contact with us.

9 PEACE COMES...

...As a Happy State of Mind

A good person's quality is to step out first because he wants to make himself and everyone around him happy.

All of us come from different backgrounds, different upbringing and different types of thoughts, but deep down inside, we all want the same things: to have a happy mind and to make the people around us happy. We want to be healthy, to be successful, to have a fruitful life and to be distant from wars, disease and difficulties.

Sometimes, we may not be able to achieve that on an external level but what is more important is to have a happy state of mind. If we have a happy state of mind, then whether we are going through a war or sitting at home watching television, our minds will be calm and filled with wisdom. We will be able to guide ourselves and others.

Having a calm and happy state of mind does not mean that you cannot shout, you don't get excited and are not allowed to scream when you're watching a ball game and your favorite team wins. Calm isn't just about being "calm." Calm is *calm abiding*, which is a state of mind that never moves from not wanting to inflict harm or engage in actions that inflict harm. A calm mind is a mind that does not ever stray or engage in actions that are motivated by bringing damage to ourselves and others, in the short and long term.

Those states of mind definitely can be achieved through education, learning and re-habituation. Everything that you can do now, everything that you are good at and are proud of, everything that you have accomplished but were not familiar with, is through habituation and learning. Everything that you know now was not easy in the beginning. Even chewing food properly was not easy when you were a small child. It is through habituation that you can now just put the food in your mouth and not have to think; you just chew. Anything that you have accomplished in your life and everything that you have in your life—conducting business, grooming, walking, talking—came from habituation.

Since habituation is the key, it is also the key to happiness and unhappiness. You can change the environment around you hundreds of times—you can change the people around you, your clothes, your country, your car and everything that you do externally, but nothing changes, although it seems like everything has changed. How many times have we switched ourselves around and seen that we fall back into the same situation?

People often feel that if they run away from a certain situation, things will change. How can things change? If we're angry with someone or with a situation, staying away from that person or situation does not take away the anger. Staying away is a symptomatic relief but it does not take away the anger. And the anger will build, grow and increase.

If you are wearing an orange shirt, then it will be an orange shirt wherever you go! Your mind is like that. If you don't transform your mind, then nothing around you will transform. If nothing around you transforms, then when you are in a difficult situation, you cannot expect that situation to dissipate or go away. Whether it is bad health, bad temper, a bad relationship or problems of disharmony, whatever problems you are having will not go away unless you remove the cause, and the cause is within you.

That cause *can* be removed, but not by mantras, rituals, prayers, miracles, Lamas touching you on your head, initiations in certain practices or visiting holy sites. That mind that creates the unhappiness in your life can only be removed when you change your habituations.

It will be a very big struggle when we try to re-habituate ourselves because we have been doing something very comfortably and naturally for many years now. If someone tells us a different way, some of us will react in anger, some of us will react with patience, some of us will react in regret and some of us will react in embarrassment—we can have all kinds of reactions. But the fact that we have a reaction means that it is irking something within us. Re-habituation of the mind is the key to all of our problems. That may sound very monumental to all of you but I am making a very logical statement.

If we look around us, if we are very honest with ourselves and examine the difficulties we have in our lives, we should begin to question where these difficulties came from. Who gave them to us? Who created them? We have to be very honest, in the silence of our rooms, alone with our minds, and we have to ask ourselves, "Was I the cause and author of all of this?" If we are honest with ourselves, we will realize that most likely we were.

The mind is very, very important. If you have a problem, please count on it that you will have more problems. If you have people problems, the chances are that you will continue to have problems with people wherever you go and with whomever you meet. Why? It cannot be that everyone is wrong and you are right all the time. It is impossible.

When someone says something negative to you that you don't like, how do you react? They may be wrong about what they have said to you, but are you right in reacting negatively? It takes two hands to clap. If they react negatively to you and you react in the same way, then you are just the same as them. But, you say, they started it. But you continued it. What's the difference?

You could work in a very negative job situation, where someone is very negative, very angry and always fighting with others. How you react to that person is how that person will react to you in the future. If you react to that person the way they react to you, you are at their level and it will get worse. If you react positively to that person, it will break the person down in time. And even if they had wanted to harm you before, they will not think about harming you anymore.

If we have problems with people at work, then we are most likely to have problems everywhere we go, with everyone we meet. If someone says that we are stingy or miserly and we move to another situation, new people will come along and say the same thing about us. If we are lazy and we don't want to do our work, then wherever we go, someone will speak up and say something about that too because who we are will manifest.

There are no shortcuts, however we are. There are no shortcuts to the path of happiness and freedom because shortcuts only offer a symptomatic treatment. They do not remove the cause.

If we are ill and there is something wrong with our bodies, blaming germs, the environment and the people who cough on us does not help. The problem is that *we* are sick and *we* have to get well. My point is not about the sickness, the people, the anger or the difficulties we have—my point is that it is time to look within, at our own minds and to see how our minds operate. If we are having the same problems again and again, we need to check what we are doing within our minds that is wrong.

You see, we can ignore the whole world and be enemies with the whole world, but it is much easier if we are friends with everyone. That is very easy if we look into our minds and say, "I am a human being, I make mistakes too and I am sorry."

The most famous mantra in Tibet is *Om Mani Peme Hung*. Each syllable in *Om Mani Peme Hung* relates to one of the six realms of *samsara* (Hell, Spirits, Animals, Human,

Demi-gods and Gods). When we recite that sincerely and well, we gain the power and ability to help and liberate all beings that exist in the six realms by the power of compassion. *Om Mani Peme Hung* is a very powerful mantra of the *Bodhisattva* of Compassion, Avalokiteshvara in Sanskrit or Chenrezig in Tibetan.

Everybody in Tibet, from little children to old people, recites this mantra. But I think there is a more powerful mantra today which is to think about letting the other person win. The words, or mantra, should be, "I am sorry." It should not be a robotic, monosyllabic, dry, cold, fake, "I am sorry." There are some people who grudgingly say, "You're right, you're right, I'm sorry! Are you happy? I apologized. I said I'm sorry, didn't I?"

When you say, "I am sorry" from the heart, it is not that you are necessarily sorry because you are wrong. Through habit, you might have done something to make someone unhappy, so you say you are sorry because someone is unhappy.

If you say this very powerful mantra—"I am sorry"—you look the other person in the eye and you mean it, it will deffuse everything. It does not mean you lose. Superficially, it may look like you have lost, you feel embarrassed and you look stupid. But look at the reaction around you—after one time, two times, three times, people will come and fold their hands and say sorry to you.

It's more effort, and you might think, "Why do I always have to be the nice guy? Why do I always have to be the good guy? Why do I always have to be the one to step out first?" Because you're the one who wants happiness. You're the one who wants to develop your mind. You're the one who wants to improve your mind. You're the one who wants to create harmony, inner peace and world peace. So those of you who want happiness, harmony and healing of your body, it starts with your mind.

You need to make the first move. If you are having a fight with a child, you can't expect the child to say, "I am sorry" or come talk to you and pat you on the back, can you? You are an adult, you are bigger! Your mind is bigger, especially if you have heard the Dharma; or if you are a good Christian, a good Buddhist, a good Jew, a good Hindu or a good atheist. You are a good person. And a good person's quality is to step out first because he wants to make himself and everyone around him happy. A good person likes to defuse the situation.

I use that example because that was the first teaching I received from His Holiness the 14th Dalai Lama in 1976 when I was only 11 years old, in Washington, New Jersey. It was about *The Eight Verses of Thought Transformation*.[1] It was a beautiful teaching and this was what His Holiness taught us. I remember it clearly.

We should make the first move and say the first thing. We should continue it and it should be a first move without agenda, pride or want of reputation; it should be from the heart *because we want happiness*. We want to be better. We want to improve our lives. And we cannot improve our lives without depending on people around us. Nobody is a rock on an island and lives on his own. We are social animals and we need to be around people.

I am giving you Buddha's teachings but they are as applicable today as they were thousands of years ago, and very logical. It is not about me sprinkling some water on you, you accepting the Buddha and being "saved." That is not going to work. None of you are going to be "saved." I'm not going to be "saved." You know how many people accept Jesus, Buddha and all that? They're not saved! Saving doesn't come from an outer source, it comes from you.

Jesus and Buddha are guides. They lead us. They inspire us, but they cannot take away our suffering and give us happiness. If they could, the world would be fabulous. I don't think Jesus or Buddha would want to lead the world the way it is now. That proves to us that they don't have the power to take away anything or give us anything. But they have the power to inspire and to teach by example, and if we follow these teachings, results will come.

10 PEACE COMES...

... When You Take a Break from Yourself

Ask yourself, at this point in your life, if you are still trying to win an argument, and if that is the most important thing to you.

There are fanatics in all religions who simply follow what someone says or follow ridiculous philosophies that have no authentic lineage or source. Ridiculous philosophies are anything that hurts another being. Any religion that teaches us to harm another—whatever the justification—is ridiculous and illogical.

We don't need religion to teach us to kill, to steal, to lie or to cheat—we are doing very well on our own! We know animals do that; as humans, we should be better. We don't need religion to teach us how to be evil and nasty, and to hurt and damage people. Religion is a science of the mind which gives us a logical explanation of our state of mind, where and how we exist. By understanding this, we re-habituate; by daily re-habituation, through meditation, prayers and contemplation, we will see a difference in our minds.

What we wish to achieve in religious—or spiritual—practice is that from last year, from the year before that or from two years before that, we see a substantial change in our mind now: we are less angry, less attached to money and we forgive more easily. Spiritual practice is not about going to places and chanting, knowing the philosophies and debating. Spiritual practice is how much our minds have changed from negative to positive.

What have we been doing for the last five years? Ten years? Fifteen years? Twenty years? *What have we been doing?* Is our mind exactly the same as it was 10 years ago? Fifteen years ago? Twenty years ago? Is our mind still angry, jealous, petty, small and complaining? Or is it more forgiving and more able to let go?

Ask yourself, at this point in your life, if you are still trying to win an argument, and if that is the most important thing to you. If you are 40, 50, 60 or 70 years old and you are still trying to win, you have wasted your life. That may have been what you needed 30, 40 or 50 years ago, but why are you still at that level? Why do you still need to win?

If you still have a hang-up that you have to be right whenever you talk to someone, you should take a break from yourself! What difference does it make what you explain? What difference does it make if people understand you or not? The important thing is, do you understand yourself? Do you understand what you are doing to yourself when you do those kinds of actions? Do you understand how much unhappiness those actions bring to yourself and others? If you do, why do you continue?

It doesn't matter if they are right or wrong. What is right or wrong is how happy or unhappy you feel. And feeling happy or unhappy is not determined solely by an outer, physical environment. It is definitely a state of mind. It is a state of mind that we can gain through development and re-habituation.

Are we still in need of the same things we needed 10, 15, 20 years ago to feel "secure"? Are we still attached or do we let go? I'm not talking about basic necessities such as food, a comfortable house and medicine when we are ill which everyone needs. I'm talking about people who still run around saying, "I need a husband. I need a wife. I need a partner. I need these clothes. I need this brand. I need this jewellery. I need this building. I need to have this title and this name... *and then I will be happy!*" Are you, at your age, still looking for these things? If, at your age, you are still looking for comfort, security and material things, then your mind has not progressed. That is how you can check whether you have used your life positively or negatively.

Some of us are still very attached to money, to form, to nice clothes or to good food. We have to check ourselves. What spiritual practice are you really doing if your hang-ups have continued up until now? Are you still making excuses? Are you still saying, "I'm going to do Dharma *when I make my million dollars*. I will do this and I will do that, *when I make my million dollars*"? Are you still breaking commitments when you make promises to people? Are you still the same?

Are you still full of anger? Are you happy being unhappy? Are you happy making other people unhappy?

If you're looking for the same thing now, you're in serious trouble. This need, this search and this perpetual drinking of salt water to quench your thirst will carry over to when you are old, when you are dying and into your next life. And the cycle goes on and on and on, it never gets cut. But you do have the power to cut it off. It is up to you.

We have to let go of whatever we have an attachment to, whatever we desire and whatever we grasp for. We have to replace it with compassion, giving, openness and trust. We have to because if we don't, what is the karma we create? What will arise? Who can help us?

Check: as the years go by, are you a source of inspiration for the people around you? When you show up, do you bring happiness to people? Is your advice adhered to or do people run away from you? Do people admire you when you speak? Or are you someone people don't pay attention to, run away from, avoid or are not interested in?

If you have so-called "wisdom" to share with others but people are not there to listen to you, that is not other people's fault. That is your fault because you have lived your life in such a way that you have chased after things that are of no significance—wine, women and song. People who have lived a while should not be asking for advice, they should be giving advice.

When we close our eyes for the last time, we should be thinking about what we have done with our lives. Have we only eaten, slept in nice places and had nice partners and friends? That's no better than an animal. What have we done for the last five years? What have we done for the last 10 years, 20 years, 30 years?

This is not something someone else asks you; this is something you ask yourself—*what have you done?* And whatever you have done, are you still looking for the same thing now? If you are still exactly as you were many years ago or if you have only changed minutely, don't sit there patting yourself on the back saying you have changed. What you have *not* changed is what will drag you down.

Each time your mind doesn't change, each time your mind exists in anger, desire, attachment and greed, it is re-habituating those negative qualities which will take you to a negative state of rebirth. Even without having to talk about a negative state of rebirth, which some of us might not accept at this time, it brings you to a negative state of existence *in this life*—with the people around you, with your spouse, with your friends and with everyone around you. No one likes to be around an angry, hateful, selfish, greedy, miserly, calculating person. No one.

Spirituality is of the spirit. What is the spirit? It is the mind. It is how much you have transformed. You have to stop making excuses for how much you have not transformed because time is short and life is short. Do you wish to reach the end of your life and go to your next life empty-handed? Think about everything you have in the bank, at your house or in investments—how will that help you at the time of death?

The next step is to do something. If you are going to be spiritual, you have to be spiritual. Spirituality is not being in a room chanting, praying and making offerings. Spirituality is about being different from what you were five years ago, 10 years ago, 20 years ago.

PART III

Peace Entails...

...The Right Program

This human core is that deep, clear nature of the mind, which is kind, giving, patient and ethical.

Most of our activities are geared more towards this life. All of us work only for this life, and think about this life and the comforts of this life. We focus on our material comforts, which can be broken down into certain categories such as reputation, financial gains, comfortable housing, friends and how people feel about us.

Most of us have a vague insecurity about how people feel about us, view us or think of us. We focus on this, dwell on it and exist on it. This is good for some people because it forms a kind of policing for them. These people are very good when they are watched and not very good when they are not watched.

This is not bad because we have been thinking this way since the time we were born, from the minute we left our mother's womb until this very moment. We care about how everyone in the world feels about us—the people we love, the people we don't love, successful people, unsuccessful people, east and west, male and female. This phenomenon is growing with the media and with the world modernizing at a tremendous pace, where we care so much about what other people think about us and what we think about other people.

In caring about what other people think about us, we sometimes lose ourselves. I find this negative because it is like someone who is forming a cult, or who preaches and teaches wrong ideas. There are cults in the middle states of America which teach that everyone who is not of a certain race, ethnicity or religion is not good. For them, anyone who does not follow their cultural identity and religious background is not good. They do not use their ideologies or politics to go higher, become better and help more people; they use these ideologies in a negative way to suppress other people who they dislike on a personal basis.

We are brought up with ingrained ideas and told to be successful for our families and for our community. This could be a good thing for some communities, such as the Chinese—everywhere in the world, you see successful Chinese people. There is a Chinatown everywhere in the world, in every country. On the negative side, that could be all that some Chinese think about—making money, looking good and trying to achieve a good reputation.

We don't actually sit there and consciously think, "I want to have a good reputation, I don't want to be embarrassed, I don't want to look bad, I don't want to be poor, I don't want to be looked down upon. When I visit my relatives or friends, I don't want to be put down." This has been programmed into some of us.

It is the same thing in other cultures. If you look at how Americans are portrayed in the movies, it is all about who has the biggest car or the biggest gun, who is the most beautiful woman or the best man, who can do something the fastest, who is the wittiest when they talk, who is the bravest or who has the greatest body. That is what they focus on.

Certain movies talk about compassion and they touch us deeply. They win awards because they reach down to our basic human nature that was with us before we took birth in this life—knowing that kindness, generosity, patience, wisdom and ethics really are the keys to harmony and happiness.

When we watch movies or see examples of these qualities, we are moved. When someone has done something wrong and they apologize from their heart, we are moved. They may have driven into our cars and shut us out of our houses but if they come to us, sincerely apologize and show regret, most of us would let go quite easily. This is because it touches the human core within us. This human core is that deep, clear nature of the mind, which is kind, giving, patient and ethical. When we hear good things, we like it.

But we have gone through programming, like a blank computer. We are a blank hard-disk and the hard-disk in that computer has been given program after program after program. We have cluttered it and its capacity has become overwhelmed. Then, the functions of the computer slow down.

Sometimes the computer just shuts down, blanks out or runs out. It is the same with people.

When we are born, we have this innate compassion within us. As we go along in life, within our individual cultures, we become re-programmed and other things become stuck into our programs: We should make money. We should be successful. We should be good-looking. We should be beautiful forever. We should look very good in front of our relatives. When we visit our relatives, we should travel in big cars. We should look this way, act this way and talk this way.

I am sure a lot of us protested (whether openly or secretly) when we were young, and thought, "Why? Why do I have to make a lot of money? Why do I have to be a doctor? Why do I have to be a lawyer? Why do I have to get married? Why do I have to have a son? Why?" After a while, our voices and our protests were drowned out, not because we were wrong or the people around us were wrong but because the overwhelming tide of forces around us—the force of materialism and the force of "I"—is very strong. When we watch movies or television programs, everyone is talking about "me." When we listen to music, everyone is singing about "me." It puts a very strong mental impression on us.

All this is programmed. We are not bad, I am not bad and you are not bad. If we say we are bad, we will not become good. We are not bad but we have been programmed incorrectly. We need to flush out that hard-disk and put in new programs, with the consistency of Windows!

...Attacking Our Afflictions

The key to happiness is taking our strongest affliction, working on it and chipping away at it over time.

Look at yourself and at your strongest affliction: the strongest thing in you that always makes you unhappy, whatever you do. Then you attack it and you break it down. For example, your strongest affliction may be always wanting to win and being a very competitive person. Then, you should learn to let the other person win. In letting other people win, you win too.

You take one mental affliction, the strongest one (you cannot take all of them at once), and you start to attack it. You should not give up. You will fail in your endeavor of attacking your strongest affliction, again and again and again. When you first ate, when you first walked, when you first left your parents or when you first worked, you also failed many times but that has brought you victory now as an independent adult. That didn't come without failures. That came with trials and tribulations.

Similarly, in your spiritual practice, don't think you can just sit down, get an image of Lama Tsongkhapa, meditate and become a Buddha overnight! People train for years to become a culinary chef or an athlete. You cannot be a culinary chef overnight, so how can you become a Buddha that quickly? That is something much greater!

If you take your strongest affliction—be it anger, desire or miserliness—and you work on it day after day after day, you *will* fail. You will go down, you will fall flat on your face, be depressed and hate yourself. But if you get up and do it again and again and again, I promise you, it will lessen.

That is how you attack your inner afflictions. I am giving you the secret here. It doesn't matter if you are white or black, from the East or West, from a Christian background, Buddhist background or no background; all those qualities are beautiful. Who cares whether you are a guy or a girl, or something in between, or both? The mind is what we are interested in. And the mind is what we are attacking.

Everyone has the right to be happy. *Everyone.* And the key to happiness is not oppressing others, taking from others, pushing others down, hurting others, taking advantage of or cheating others. That is not the key to happiness. The key to happiness is taking our strongest affliction, working on it and chipping away at it over time. When we chip away at it over time, we will see it lessen. When that lessens, the reactions that would have arisen from that mind will also lessen.

If, for example, we usually react in anger 10 times a day, then we should cut it down to reacting only nine times a day; then eight times a day; then seven times a day. With time, it will lessen. When we act less from anger, our reactions to that anger will lessen, and the counter-reactions from others to us will also lessen. When they lessen, we will experience some happiness and more peace. There will be more harmony and we will be more in control. That is the secret. That is the key to practising.

The more we do not change this mind, the more we will react from it. And it becomes solidified and stronger. With this type of mind, we will only create more unhappiness and make more enemies. We will have more people and more beings to fight off. It becomes very tiresome in the end.

To counter this and to encourage our practice, we should study what the Buddha achieved in his Enlightenment and apply it. We should apply different methods, and acknowledge that we will fail many times.

It does not matter whether you are depressed or unhappy. If you fail, you should get up and do it again and again. You have to do it again, that's life. If you don't like to put in the effort, then don't wash yourself, because tomorrow you will get dirty again. Don't wash your hair, because it will get dirty again next week. Why wash yourself? Why brush your teeth? They're going to get dirty again!

Everything arises from the mind. Therefore, if you apply this practice to your mind, all situations will change. Your mind is what you will take with you when you die. When you die and you take a rebirth, you will continue where your mind has left off. If you are an angry, hateful, childish person, you will be reborn as that and continue what you have been doing; maybe not even as a human being. If, on the other hand, you have developed your mind to a certain stage (through meditation and practice, for example), then when you take rebirth again, you will act from that state and that level of mind.

13 PEACE ENTAILS...

...Not Blaming Others

If you have called for a taxi and the taxi is late, would you scold the car or the driver? If negative things happen to us and we scold others, it is like scolding the car.

In Buddhist practice, it is very, very important not to blame, accuse, point fingers or say that everything is others' fault. This counters the law of cause and effect. If it counters the law of cause and effect, then the fundamental basis of Buddhism is not strong in our minds.

The fundamental method for countering our blame of others, our pointing fingers at others, or thinking that something is another person's fault and not taking responsibility for it, is to understand the workings of karma—cause and effect—meditating on karma and accepting that karma is the basis of all our unhappiness.

If we meditate on cause and effect, our anger will lessen. Many of us experience and express tremendous anger. Many of us, over the years, have shown so much anger to others that people are afraid or find it difficult to be near us. In many cases, people do not want to be near us, making us angrier and angrier. When we keep blaming others, our anger intensifies and we find ourselves with fewer and fewer friends. Eventually, we are not beneficial to ourselves or to others.

To counter their anger, people find solace in therapy, philosophies, meditation on lights, acupuncture or mantras. But the best way to counter anger is to take responsibility. How do we take responsibility? By believing one hundred percent in the law of cause and effect, or karma.

If we believe in cause and effect, we will not be angry. Every time we get angry, there is a message we show others: that we do not believe in cause and effect because we are blaming someone else. People with tremendous anger, people who are very impatient all the time, people who are not able to control their mind, or bring it down to listening to or applying the Dharma—due to impatience, anger or any of these obstructions—have not meditated on the law of cause and effect. If we really believe in karma, we will realize that everything arises as a result of ourselves. There is nothing to blame, begrudge or nag.

In order to counter anger, we have to meditate on the workings of karma, and how it affects our lives. If we take away all the trappings of Tibetan, Japanese, Chinese, Thai, Mahayana or Theravada Buddhism—the clothes, the altars, the statues, the temples, the decoration and the style—it boils down to one simple item: karma. That is what was taught by the Buddha.

When we are frustrated with others, we blame others, or we want to talk to others about our problems; when we do not want to amend, take care of or deal with our problems, and we always blame others, look at others, accuse others and get angry, it is a clear, direct, open indication that we have not taken refuge from our heart. If we have, we will believe one hundred percent in karma. If we believe in karma, we will never blame others. This is because we understand that if we are the cause, they are just the environmental factors for this result to happen.

The solution to our problems—such as anger, impatience, miserliness, greed, unhappiness, restlessness—is meditation on karma and the realization of karma. If we realize karma, we will not run away anymore. If we believe in karma, we will not become angry or show an angry face, even to the people who have hurt us. If we believe in karma, we will push ourselves to become better people, strive and not sit there reticent, lazy or disinterested, without goals or the willingness to push ourselves.

If you have called for a taxi and the taxi is late, would you scold the car or the driver? If negative things happen to us and we scold others, we blame others and we show anger and speak harsh words to others, it is like scolding the car. Actually, the driver is at fault. The driver is ourselves.

If we meditate on karma and we believe in karma, our attachments, our impatience and stinginess will all go away or lessen. Our impatience and pointing fingers at other people will also go away because if we meditate on karma and its effects, we will realize that we are the driver; we will realize that we are actually in control.

If we are in control, we must *take* control, by taking responsibility. If we say, "The traffic was bad, it was this person's fault, that person talked like that, I have to go here, I have to do this," we are always putting the responsibility onto others. When we do this, we cannot gain attainments because we have not accepted the fundamental practice of taking refuge in Dharma, which is to understand cause and effect, and to realize that all things are created from our mind, directly and indirectly. All people, all environments, all situations are created from our mind.

If we believe in karma, we will never be sneaky, we will not be ill-mannered, we will not wish to harm others, we will do our work conscientiously and a hundred percent from our heart. Because we realize that *we* are the drivers.

If we are full of anger, then we will always blame others and we will always be looking for therapies, medicines, places and environments to calm down our anger. Those methods can be beneficial temporarily but it cannot be beneficial in the long term because that anger will continue to grow and grow. Do you want to reduce your anger? Be your own therapist. Meditate on cause and effect. Meditate and realize you are the driver. Do not blame people or say, "I'm impatient, I'm angry, I don't want to do this and that, it's their fault, it's this person's fault, it's that person's fault."

Saying that you will take responsibility and leaving it at that is not good enough. You have to think of *how* to take responsibility—by the philosophy, thinking and understanding of karma. If we believe in and understand the fundamental basis of karma, then many, many, many things in us will calm down.

Buddhist philosophy is very, very powerful for healing the world today because it does not put the responsibility on an outer deity and it does not blame others. It makes us take responsibility. Whether there is a God or not is not Buddha's concern and not our concern at this time. Our concern is that we take responsibility based on the truth of cause and effect—we are the driver and we get to the destination we want to get to.

If we believe in that and we live our life according to that philosophy, things will be very, very different. If we choose to believe in that, and then add a God theory, that is also wonderful. Whether we believe in God or not, the issue here is actually about taking responsibility.

If the issue was about believing in God, then all the people who believe in God would never make trouble for others, never engage in violence, speak negative words, cheat or lie. The people who believe in God would be very peaceful and happy. If it was enough to just believe in God to find world peace, personal peace and relational peace, then simply saying "I believe in God," or going to a place that accepts God will bring about peace for everything. We can see from overwhelming evidence in the world that simply believing in God does not bring about that result.

We must think deeper. Whether we wish to believe in God or not is our choice. At this time, what is more important than believing in God is believing in ourselves. When we believe we are the drivers, we will take responsibility for our actions and for the results. We will not blame others.

If we want to drive the car of miserliness, we will reach the destination that it brings us to. If we want to drive the car of anger, we will also reach the destination of anger. Wherever we want to drive to is up to us. We are the driver.

We might, for example, use and abuse other people's bodies for our own pleasure and not care about what happens to them. We might use them like a packet of cigarettes, just smoking and throwing them out, and not thinking of them as conscious beings with feelings and karma, who can be hurt. Sometimes when we use other people's bodies, throw them out and hurt them, we contribute towards opening up some latent karma in them that becomes violent, angry or very twisted.

Then, they might react in violence, pain or anger. This means we were the cause for that karma to open in them. If we open that karma in them, and they hurt because of that, the karma will come back to us. In the future, we will continue to do this to others, again and again and again.

In this case, using other people's bodies is the car we drive and that is the destination we will arrive at. It could be that we are reborn as an animal or a spirit in our next life[1]; it could be that no one will respect us and we will have no friends in this life, and that violence and disrespect will follow us wherever we go. If that is the car we want to drive, then that is the destination we will arrive at.

On the other hand, if we are driving a car that is going in the right direction, we will go further in that direction. If we are going in the wrong direction, we can turn our car around and go in the right direction—if we believe in karma. Who can make us believe in that? Ourselves. And we can believe in that by meditating on all the problems and difficulties we have created for ourselves and others.

The solution is not to lock ourselves in a room and hide away. The solution is to face these problems by taking responsibility and by doing the most difficult thing we could ever do—to realize that all problems arise from ourselves and that there is no point in expressing anger in any way, shape or form, at any time.

If we meditate on the law of cause and effect, immediately, we will see ourselves with more patience. If, for example, we were afraid to say or do things that would destroy our reputation or happiness, or take away our wealth, status or free time, all those fears would dissipate if we meditated on cause and effect. Why will it go away? Because when we meditate on cause and effect, we will realize what brings about positive effects. If we meditate on what causes good effects, then we will want to create the causes to bring about more of these good effects.

If we believe, trust, meditate and focus on cause and effect, anger will dissipate, our blaming of others will be reduced, happiness will arise, patience will arise and enthusiastic effort to do positive things for others will arise because we will only want to create the causes for happiness. The cause of happiness is focusing on others.

...Not Complaining

If you keep complaining, you are not helping anyone; you will create more animosity and you will chase people away. Stop getting angry at people and stop ignoring people. Take responsibility.

If we are in a difficult, nasty, ugly situation, we should be very happy—we are purifying our karma. We should not complain anymore about our friends, husbands, wives, family or difficult situations.

You know why you shouldn't complain? First of all, it does not get better if you complain. Secondly, it hurts people. Thirdly, *you* picked the situation! *You* had the monster kids, nobody asked you to have the kids. *You* married the monster husband or the monster wife, so why are you complaining?

Let go. After today, go and make friends with these people, and keep them as friends. After today, if anybody disturbs your mind, change *your* mind and transform. If you want to be a Dharma practitioner, if you want to receive the higher teachings, if you wish for the Gurus to live long, you must let go.

How do you let go? Realize that you created the karma for this, and you have experienced the karma. Watch it and let go. The next time someone disappoints you and hurts you, let go. Then, when the next time comes along, the next person comes along or the next situation comes along, you will be able to let go, more and more and more each time.

You think, "But they are going to hurt me more." No, *you* hurt yourself more. Why do you hurt yourself more? Because *you* hold on. Let go. If you are my student, let go. Don't embarrass me anymore in public. If you are a Buddhist, let go. If you are 120 years old, and you are going to pass on any day now, let go. If you are 20 years old, and the people around you are 120 years old, you had better let go because any time soon, *they* will pass on!

What do you let go of? Your anger, ignoring others, expectations, projections and how you feel others should be. Let go. If you believe in the Buddha, let go. If you like to make offerings on the altar, let go. When you teach Dharma to others or to your family and friends, and you want it to have power, let go. If you don't, then no one will listen to you when you teach and explain, and you will not be able to bring anyone closer to the Dharma. Even though you know the Dharma, you will have no power because you do not practice.

So let go. If you love your mother (and you should), let go. If you are a real Buddhist, let go. Last but not least, if you are a human being, let go because we have to live together. We have to work together and we have to have harmony.

You might ask why *they* don't let go. Because they didn't have anyone to tell them what's wrong with not letting go. No one taught them the Dharma, no one gave them knowledge. So *you* should let go, not them, because they do not have the merits or the karma to know about letting go. If a child jumps up and down in a tantrum, and the mother jumps up and down too, wouldn't that look stupid? It would be better if the mother told the child not to jump up and down, and not to behave like that. If the mother jumped up and down, and the child told the mother not to jump up and down, how would that look?

If you don't let go, you can tap dance for a few years and sing, "I hate you! I'm angry with you! I ignore you!" One day, you will not be able to tap dance anymore, and *they* are going to tap dance on you! If you don't let go, *you* will become depressed. If you don't let go, *you* will become angrier. If you don't let go, more people will come to *you* and *you* will hate them all the more. If you don't let go, you send your mother and your father to "hell." They have to live knowing they have produced a monster who creates negative karma. If you keep holding on to your anger, you will send your mother and father to hell, on earth and after. They will look at their son or daughter and wonder why they are behaving like that.

Do you want to practice Dharma or do you want to practice *samsara*? How long do you want to have anger? How long do you want to hold on to your concepts? How long do you want to hold on to the way you think things should be and thinking, "They're like that, which is why I'm like this"?

Anger is not shouting, screaming or slapping people. Anger is holding on. You might shout and slap someone but it is over and finished in the next minute. The next day, you are able to talk to them nicely and kindly again, and apologize for what you did. Then you feel light. But if the next day, the next week, the next month you are still holding on, you don't talk to the person, you ignore him and you make many enemies, then you will bring your spiritual energy down, you will become depressed, alone, single and no one will respect you, no matter how beautiful, handsome, rich and educated you are.

No one will go near you because you are full of anger. Anger is your enemy. You heal anger by taking responsibility. Stop asking everyone why you are born like this, why you are here or why you are like that. Listen to what Lord Buddha said, not what you say. Who's right? You or the Buddha?

If people have hurt you and caused you anger, realize that you have done something to them before. If your anger arises, don't react to it. This means that you do not carry out the anger. When you do not carry out the anger—even after two or three years—the anger will dissipate because you are not feeding it. A fire cannot keep burning without oil, can it? If you are still feeling angry now, it is as if your fire is still there because you keep thinking about it and feeding it with oil. Why do you focus on the one person who has hurt you and who you are angry with? Aren't there many people you are *not* angry with? Think about the many people who haven't done anything to you.

To get rid of anger, you have to get rid of the ego. It is not just about getting rid of anger; it is about eliminating wrong self-projection and the self-cherishing mind. As long as you have the self-cherishing mind, you will have anger. So don't talk about anger, talk about the self-cherishing mind and work on that. When you work on that, you will realize that it is not about the person who makes you angry; it is about yourself and how you get rid of the anger.

When you finish reading these teachings, take a vow not to complain anymore. Every time you want to complain, control your mouth. That includes controlling yourself from writing it down. Don't be smart and think that even though you do not say anything, you can make others read your written complaints!

If you mess up, don't worry. There were many hours you didn't mess up. Congratulate yourself on that. If you mess up, push yourself the next day. When do you give up? You never give up. Do you want to go back to what you were? Do you want to be unhappy? Do you want to waste the rest of your life until they bury you in the ground being a complainer or do you want to leave a mark of kindness behind?

If you complain 50 times a day, then cut it down to 48. Then make it 47, 46, 45, etc. Remember, you created the karma to be in this situation and to have this rebirth. You picked. You made the choice. You did it. You have to experience it. It is very simple. Don't complain. Don't blame others. Take responsibility. Then your anger lessens, you begin to accept people, your sour face becomes sweet and it becomes a much better life.

When you stop complaining, you will find that people change. Why? Because *you* change. When you stop complaining, your anger will become less. Why will your anger become less? The anger comes from you, therefore *you* have to do something about it, not other people. Even if the 20 people who made you angry say they are sorry, there will be another 20 people next year, next month or next week, in another place, who will make you angry. If you don't change, people will keep making you angry. If you change, people cannot make you angry, wherever you are. Then you start living.

You are not living right now by being angry, by ignoring people or by having a lot of sadness and depression. You are not living, you are dying. So you need to live and you can achieve this by letting go of expectations. Stop thinking that things should be this way or that way, and questioning when it doesn't happen the way you think it should. Let go. I promise you, life will change.

I am not asking you to prostrate in front of the Buddha or to come and kiss my feet. I am asking you to take refuge in the Dharma and surrender—take responsibility by accepting what happens to you and improving yourself. Dharma is determination based on a clear perception of reality. At this level, having a clear perception of reality is about taking responsibility for the bad things that happen in life, as well as taking credit for the good things. We like to take credit for the good things that happen but we don't want to take responsibility for the bad things!

Taking responsibility is a nice phrase but what does it really mean? It means that you do not blame others. Even if someone is at fault, you should not blame them and you should not point fingers. If you practice not blaming others, then whether someone is right or wrong, you will not blame them. There could be times when you come across someone who is sincerely in the right but because you are in the habit of blaming others, you could hurt them. Instead, if you train yourself not even to blame people who are wrong, then the people who deserve your compassion will also benefit.

This is about being happy. Can it be achieved? Yes, it can. You can achieve happiness if you take responsibility. Your mother makes mistakes, your father makes mistakes, your friends make mistakes, your husband and wife make mistakes, your sisters and brothers make mistakes. Yes, everyone makes mistakes. But so do you. Whose mistake is bigger? It depends on your perception and what angle you are looking from. The angle from which you look at a situation is proportionate to how big the mistake is.

If you tell someone that his shirt is ugly, some people would thank you for telling them and change their shirt. Some people would not go to the party with you anymore because they have a big ego trip and feel completely down and depressed. How big the problem is depends on your perception.

Accept. Acceptance does not mean you have to stay in a deep, dark hole. Acceptance means you find Buddhist methods—human determination, respect, understanding and letting go—to transform the difficulties with patience and acceptance. You do not have to be a Buddhist to practice Buddhist principles. In fact, these are humanistic principles.

So how do I make myself happy?

A. Stop putting projections on other people.

B. Stop complaining. Just shut up. Every time you want to complain, recite the "mantra" *Om Shut*

Up Hung Phet[1] instead! You don't want to do mantras, *sadhanas*, prayers and prostrations because you don't have time or you can't push yourself. That's okay. What you can do instead is to *not complain*. You can do that any time, 24 hours a day. If you keep complaining, you are not helping anyone; you will create more animosity and you will chase people away. Stop getting angry at people and stop ignoring people. Take responsibility.

C. Stop expecting others to change; *you* change. Stop expecting other people to talk to you first; *you* talk to them first. Stop expecting them to be a better person; *you* be a better person! *You* do it! You believe in Buddha and you want to be a Dharma practitioner, so you change yourself.

Don't ask why the world isn't changing. The whole world is looking at you asking why *you* aren't changing. What's easier? To change the whole world or to change yourself? If you keep trying to change the whole world, you will be fighting for the rest of your life with anger. Change yourself. Transform yourself. It is very simple but very deep and very profound.

15 PEACE ENTAILS...

...Cutting the Cycle of Catch 22

Taking responsibility is not about who is right or wrong. Taking responsibility is about finding a solution.

No one gives us suffering. No one has put suffering in front of us. We create the suffering because of our wrong view and our wrong perception of what is going on around us. This could be wrong perception of a person or a message, of what is going on around us or of what is being communicated, and our reaction to that wrong perception.

When we react to that wrong perception, more wrong perception arises. For example, we may have spent a lot of time on a favorite shirt in our favorite color; we have taken care of it, sent it to the cleaners, dry-cleaned it and done everything we could to maintain it. Someone might then come along and say to us, "You know, that shirt is nice but you should wear this color and this type of shirt instead because it will make you look much better."

That person may have been trying to be open by sharing his opinion with us and he did not mean to criticize. But we might have a wrong perception. When we were very young, we might have been a fashion victim and been criticised about our clothes for a long, long time. Recently, we became fashion conscious, so if anyone says anything to us about our clothes, we become highly sensitive, although it is not a big deal to anyone else.

We shout, we scream, we say, "I don't want to be his friend anymore, I don't want to be near him anymore." We take a very small situation, blow it out of proportion and make it very big.

You might call it miscommunication. I like to call it misperception. What people say to us and what people perceive of us is completely different from what we perceive within the same situation. How we act and react to the other person is dependent on how narrow or broad our mind is. If our mind is very narrow—due to the lack of exposure, lack of study and, mostly, the lack of application of Dharma—we will be very sensitive and get very angry, we will hold grudges, always show a sour face and always show ourselves not to be wrong.

Wrong perception is based on wrong experiences. Wrong experiences arise from wrong perception. Wrong perception is again fed by wrong experience. This becomes a Catch 22 situation. It goes back and forth, back and forth, becoming stronger and stronger. Most of us operate on wrong perception fed by wrong experience. What is a wrong experience? When someone tells us that our shirt could be changed to something better and we become very insulted or hurt by the comment. This is because previous experiences have taught us that that is the way we should react: we reacted this way before so we must also react this way now.

The danger in this is that while we may have gotten away with acting a certain way before, the people or situations are now different. Since the people and situations are different, we might lose many opportunities if we continue to act the way we did before: friends, husbands, wives and relatives could all be lost. How we reacted to a situation in the past cannot be applied now.

People have a lot of anger because in the past, people acted, said or did things to them that "helped" create this anger. However, although they are not with their parents, their relatives, their ex-wives or ex-husbands anymore, they still have this anger within them. They are not in that situation anymore but that situation is still living on in them; they are still reacting to new people now as they did before.

For example, a very nasty customer might come into a store that we own. He fights, so we fight back. When he goes away, we still feel very angry. If another customer comes into the store, we might react in the same way even if the new customer doesn't do anything to us and is innocent. But because we are angry, we look at the new person and think that he will probably treat us badly, put us down and say negative things again. That next customer might have bought something from our store, but because we were giving out negative vibes or showed an angry face, we lost that chance.

We always hear about people who feel sorry for themselves, who think and say, "When I was little, my mother used to scold me. When I was in school, they used to treat me like this. My father always talked to me in this way. My brother always spoke to me in that way." They always refer to what happened to them as an excuse to continue with what they are doing now.

In Western psychology, our parents or our experiences as a child trap us. In that kind of psychology, you have to blame someone; you have to make someone the "enemy." You have to push the psychology and the responsibility onto someone else. "It was my mother. It was my father. It was my schoolmates. It was my brothers and sisters. I'm competitive, I cheat and I lie to win because my brothers and sisters always did well and I couldn't. I got into the habit of lying and cheating to compete with them." In psychology, we start crying, we break down and we go through many therapies.

Some people say, "Every time I failed, my mother was very, very fierce with me. Now, I am afraid to fail." We pin the blame on our mother. We do not hate her because we know she is not bad but psychology tells us to pin the blame on our mother.

I have watched many programs about serial killers. When they profile them or when they go through hypnotherapy, they say that they were abused by their uncle or a neighbor during their childhood, and they begin to cry. They pin the blame on the fact that someone touched them. It is a very common excuse in America to say, "I was touched." When you say "I was touched," it becomes "permissible" to sexually abuse other people. It seems to be a catchword now. But to understand what I am talking about psychologically is not enough. We have to apply it.

I grew up with a lot of anger in my life when I was a child. My foster mother, with respect to her, was filled with anger (please do not think I am putting her down. I do not mean to). She went through World War Two, and suffered poverty and upheaval of her home twice. She had to be an immigrant twice, she was uneducated, and had to struggle and work in factories her whole life. She was a very, very intelligent lady and quite kind but she suffered a lot.

She had a lot of anger because she had a lot of pain and rejection when she was a child. She would walk out of her house during the wars in Eastern Europe and there would be soldiers and corpses all over the roads. She would be made to go out to find food for the family and it was a very scary experience—imagine a young, pretty, innocent girl going through all these corpses and dead people to steal bread and food. She had to become very hard and very cold to go through this.

There were people putting her down, soldiers catching her and people spitting on her. She was also in a concentration camp when she was very young in Germany. She experienced everything the Jewish people experienced in those concentration camps. I found out about all of this later, that her past experiences were what made her very angry and hard.

I remember, during my childhood, that in her moment of anger, when she was angry with someone, she would see nothing but her anger. She would avoid and ignore that person for weeks and months. She had been ignoring some of our relatives for a year before she died. She was upset about something small when she went to their wedding, so she threw a huge tantrum and left the wedding. She upset all the relatives, the crowd and the hundreds of people. She ignored that side of her family—her younger sister and nieces—for a whole year before she passed away.

She lived like that that for many, many years and I took on some of her characteristics. She was my example because I respected her very much. I learned that anger from her: I learned that when I was angry with someone, I should ignore them, not talk to them or look at them, and wait for them to come to me first. I did that in America for many years (though not on an extreme or evil level)—I ignored people and I avoided people. There were some people I ignored for six months to a year.

Later, when I thought about it, and when I attended Dharma classes with my Lama, Geshe Tsultim Gyeltsen in his center in Los Angeles, I realized that what I was doing was exactly what my foster mother did to me and to other people.

I wasn't healed because I was blaming her, I was telling people it was her fault, saying that that was how she trained me, what she taught me, what she said, and that that was all I knew. When you go through Western psychotherapy, you stay right there. You release yourself and the blame from yourself by putting it on an object that hurt you: your uncle touched you, your mother didn't give you attention, your father was never around, your aunt abused you or you were called fat and stupid in school. You blame your uncle, your mother and father, your aunt and your school. You blame everyone. You stop at that level and you never truly heal.

In Buddhism, you go to the next level—you take responsibility. You think like this: "There are so many mothers and fathers on this planet. Why did I take rebirth with that parent? Why?" In Buddhist theory, you go back to cause and effect, which is that you created the karma to be born in this kind of environment, to experience this kind of experience. In Buddhist psychology, when you don't blame your mother, father, sister, school or environment anymore, you will be free. You realize that they are the environmental cause, the temporary cause for you to experience what you experience. The real cause was your karma to be born in that situation.

You think instead, "Yes, it is my school; yes, it is my aunt; yes, it is my environment," but you also ask, "Why am I in this situation?" You realize it is because of cause and effect, and that you created that karma. You have a choice now: to keep blaming the other person for your depression and anger, for your lack of success and for being a loser, or to take responsibility.

My teacher, Geshe-la, told me to call my foster mother and tell her that I was sorry. I had run away from my home[1] in New Jersey to Los Angeles and he told me to call her and say sorry. I said, "What!? I'm the one who got beaten, I'm the one who got screamed at, I was the one who was slapped, hurt and abused all the time by her for many years. Why do I need to apologize?"

He said, "Because you need to advance in your practice."

I said, "What do you mean? Why should I apologize to her? It's not my fault!"

He said, "Because you don't look only at the negative things your mother did. You also have to look at the positive. You're here, someone fed you and gave you a home. You're here in our center and that is because of your mother's kindness. Call her and say you're sorry for the things you said to her and the things you thought about her."

I said, "She's not going to take my call."

He said, "Never mind. You call her. Even if she doesn't take your call, you tried. At least when you pray and when you do your *sadhana*, it comes from your heart, it is real."

So I called her. I said I loved her and that I was sorry. She hung up on me. She told me she disowned me, I would get nothing and I would have nothing. She disowned me. It was very painful.

But I am glad I called her. Now that she has passed away, I think to myself, "Thank goodness I did that." From my side, I cut the karma off to meet her again in the future to have a negative relationship. She might meet me again and try to harm me but I will not harm her back. The karma from me to her is cut, because I said I was sorry and I meant it.

After I called her, I went to Geshe-la and told him I'd made the call. He said, "Very good. Now make me a cup of tea. Get lost." I didn't get any praise, I didn't get a pat on the back. It was so emotional for me, it was so difficult because I was abused by my foster mother for years, I ran away three times, I slept outside, I almost starved to death, I was beaten, I was held at gunpoint. I finally ran away and hitchhiked from New Jersey to New York, and from New York to California. But I realized at that time, when I was about 16 or

17, that if I didn't apologize to her, I would hold on. If I held on, how could I do my *sadhanas* and retreats? How could I go to India and be a monk? A monk is supposed to be kind.

In Buddhist philosophy, you go to the next level and take responsibility for what happens to you and around you. That is what I did when I said sorry to my foster mother. It was to say, "I'm sorry for thinking that it was your fault. It is my karma to be born in this situation."

I think when I said I was sorry, it was the Buddhist way of healing. I have no regrets. I didn't do anything wrong. But when I looked deeper, when I listened more deeply to the teachings from my Lama, I realized that I created the karma to be born there. Now, when I come across this kind of situation I can handle it very well.

If you say "I'm sorry" and really mean it, what are you actually sorry for? You are sorry for your wrong view, the way you acted and the way you hurt people. Do you think you are always right and everyone else is wrong? It cannot be.

Instead, when you think, "I created the karma to be in this situation; I have this family, I have these friends and I am in this place because of karma," then you will take responsibility. When you take responsibility, you will start to heal. I promise you that. When you take responsibility, you will stop blaming others. When you stop blaming others, your anger will lessen. When your anger lessens, many things will become easier.

Taking responsibility is not about who is right or wrong. Taking responsibility is about finding a solution. Why should you say you are sorry or take responsibility? Because you know the Dharma; because you are depressed, you are sad, you are angry, you are wasting your life and time, you are always running away, escaping and avoiding, and you don't want to listen to people who tell you things you don't like. That is why you should say you are sorry and let go.

I am not the best person but I did grow up wanting to benefit others. I did grow up knowing about mental pain and about the scars of war. I did grow up knowing about people who are hurt; I grew up knowing that we should forgive people like that, that they suffer more than we do, and that they deserve our compassion and love, not our pity. I knew we shouldn't add to their pain and that by us saying sorry, they have one less enemy. By saying sorry to my foster mother, I was accepting my situation. And when you accept your situation, you transform.

PART IV

Peace Is Transforming...

...Experiences

All the experiences we have fade into a dream but what we do during those experiences and our reactions to the people around us do not.

Everything that you have experienced from the time you were born until now and many of the details of what has happened cannot be remembered anymore. You can no longer recall much. In fact, when someone talks or reminds you of something that happened in the past, you ask if it really happened. Sometimes, you remember only a few bits and pieces.

Even the things that we threw fits about when we were children—when we threw our bottles down, screamed and hit our mothers and fathers—were so serious while they were happening but are now just a distant dream. However, the habits and tendencies associated with the bratty little kids that we were—for example, our habit of throwing tantrums—are not forgotten. When we grow up into adults and we are still temperamental, difficult and full of anger, people who know us will say, "Yes, they were like that as a child."

The experiences of whatever we do will fade away and disappear, and eventually they will not matter anymore. In fact, by next week you will not even remember that you had read this. For some of us, what was taught and explained here will already be forgotten by next week. This is not an insult—unfortunately, it is just the way our mind works. We experience the experiences we have, whether pleasant or unpleasant, like we are watching a drama or a play. During the play, the experience is very intense if the actors and actresses are very good. They make us cry, they make us laugh, they make us feel anxious—we feel real because our minds become totally absorbed in the play. However, when the play is over, we come back to reality. We know that it was just a play and that it was just made up of actors and actresses.

Sometimes we read about actors and actresses and what they do in those bad, little gossip magazines. We like those magazines for a few reasons. Even I like them! I read all about who is having what liposuction, who broke up with whom, who is with whom, who is suspected of this and that.

One of the reasons we like those magazines, and we read them and are interested in them, is that when we see these actors and actresses on the screen, they portray a certain character—a very good person or a very rotten, evil person. We begin to identify the person with that character. When we read these magazines and discover that they do not match the characters they play on screen, we find it interesting.

For example, we may see an actress play the part of a nun where she is very saintly. On screen, we see her as wonderful, saintly and fabulous but we might then read in a magazine that she has been divorced four times. We might react and think, "What kind of nun is that?!" and we are intrigued because it does not match the character we have associated her with. We like that. That is something subconscious in all of us.

Similarly, things that happen to us, good and bad, are like a play or a show. Think about it. No matter how much intensity we put into the experience, the experience will pass and what has happened will pass. The person we had the good or bad experience with will pass and go away, and they will fade into a dream. Think about relationships, and the friends and people you knew 10 years ago, five years ago, two years ago, one year ago. You cannot remember some of them anymore; there are some you don't even wish to remember.

They fade, and even the people we have relationships with now and in the future may just become memories. All the experiences we have fade into a dream but what we do during those experiences and our reactions to the people around us do not fade; they do not just remain as memories.

For example, someone might cut us off in traffic and immediately, we aggressively chase after them. In a short while, that chase will be over but the *action* of anger—of chasing them and wanting to extract revenge by scaring them—does not go away. We reinforce our anger, we experience the anger and we feel familiar with it. It is even worse when there are no immediate repercussions because we can then engage in it again and again and again, until it becomes something very serious. Whatever we have done that is hurtful and damaging to the other person is reflected and transformed into karma; that karma remains and that karma goes on.

The horrible aspect about karma is that it multiplies daily. The next horrible thing about karma is that it comes back to us. Therefore, whatever we have done to other people—our parents, our girlfriends and boyfriends, our friends and acquaintances—will pass, and although we might not remember what the experience was, the action and repercussions of the experience will remain.

It is okay if you do not believe in karma because I am not here to force you to believe it. If you do not believe in karma, then believe in this—the action stays because you reinforce it. For example, some people can be very attached to a relationship and put all their energy into it. However, the relationship will eventually fade and break down, and all the energy and time that was put into the relationship will go with it. There are some people who try to recapture or retrieve that relationship but it can never be like it was before—the karma for it is gone.

Some of us might have a good relationship but choose to end it; before long, we want another good relationship, achieve it and then end it again. We have this power of ending relationships or of not wanting to maintain our relationships. The result is inevitable—there will come a time when our karma builds up and someone will do the same back to us. It will happen at a time when we will not be able to tolerate it—if we do not have Dharma or a strong, psychologically stable background, we will not be able to bear it. We may commit suicide, do something violent, hurt someone or ourselves, or become vengeful—we become capable of doing a lot of things. Therefore, even so-called "good" relationship experiences can end up badly because they reinforce something that is not real.

17 PEACE IS TRANSFORMING...

...Misunderstandings

We need to create transformation today, so we can create new ideas about ourselves tomorrow.

From a Buddhist perspective, we believe that whatever experience we have—whether positive or negative—it is how we react during and immediately after the experience that creates karma. On a worldly, psychological level, we believe that when the experience is over, what we have done during that experience—the way we behave and talk, and our body language—creates a reputation for us.

This reputation precedes the actual results to come, and causes people to form preconceived ideas of who, what and how we are. Whether these preconceived notions are true or not does not matter—people experience us as we experience them.

For example, you may normally be sloppy and unaware, and you forget things; you may not pay attention and are not alert; you may be full of anger and react negatively; you may be irresponsible, lazy and like to hide behind your tears; you may normally forget to fulfil your commitments. Or, you may be a person who is normally very responsible, very kind and gentle; you may be very skilful and enthusiastic to help. However you are, if you are a certain way over a long period of time, those attitudes or actions form preconceived ideas about you and those preconceptions create your reputation. That reputation of you, whether true or false, creates more conceptions about you in others' minds. And that conception is what usually hurts us. We are always complaining and saying things like, "I'm misunderstood. People don't understand me." We spend a lot of time explaining, justifying and talking about ourselves to others. However, when we look at ourselves deeply, we have no results.

We have no results but we are very eloquent in explaining *why* we have no results in our life or in our spiritual practice. Why is it that we can explain why we have no results but lack an answer to do something to change it? Since we know why we have no results, we must also know the antidote. If we do not know of an antidote, there are two paths available to us— find one in the Buddha or find one in a friend who has wisdom. We should not stick to our narrow views, actions and ways of thinking because it brings us nowhere. It has brought us nowhere so far.

Therefore, if we have bad relationships with our parents, our spouses, our friends or people we meet and we are constantly "misunderstood," we need to understand that we have created that reputation for ourselves, directly or indirectly. We need to stop always explaining and justifying. We might even have created that reputation for ourselves on a subconscious level. There are some of us who think that we have been very good in this life. In our ignorance and darkness, we might believe that we have not done anything wrong and that it is unfair of people to think badly of us and accuse us. There is a reason and a cause for that—we might be acting in situations without consciously realizing *how* we act.

Yes, people might misunderstand us because of the way we do things, but should we spend the rest of our lives explaining how "good" we are? Or do we live in a world with a lot of other sentient beings and should, therefore, learn to accommodate their needs and ways of thinking?

What we also need to understand is that even if we have not done very much in this life, the habituation may have come from previous life. (Past-life regression therapy is not just a Buddhist concept; it is also very, very big in the West these days.)

If we have difficulty with certain people or situations, or even if we are not doing anything and people still accuse us or have certain views about us, we have to ask ourselves what we have done to create that misconception. People's preconceptions and notions about us arise from the way we have reacted to experiences in the past—if people think we are lazy or we shirk responsibility, we have to ask ourselves what we may have done to create that idea.

We have two ways of dealing with this situation—if we *have* done something to create people's preconceptions about us, we should remain silent and change. If we have not, instead of trying to justify what we have done, we should realize that by the power of cause and effect, we may have created that perception from our previous lives. That habituation started somewhere, whether a year ago, two years ago, three years ago, a lifetime ago or 10 lifetimes ago. It did start somewhere.

The wrong way to deal with the situation would be to spend the rest of our lives defending ourselves, putting all of our energy into telling people how right (but misunderstood!) we are, and not putting our energy into transforming ourselves. We only have a certain amount of energy and time. If we put all our energy and time into explaining everything around us, we might finally justify ourselves but we would have achieved nothing by the end of our lives.

If we have such a limited amount of energy and time, would it not be better to put it towards transforming ourselves, so that the preconceived ideas about us will slowly crumble away? The change would not be as fast as when we explain and justify ourselves directly, but the change will be more effective and will last longer.

We begin to transform ourselves now by learning the Dharma, listening to the teachings, contemplating and meditating. We need to contemplate and incorporate the Dharma into our lives to create transformation today, so we can create new ideas about ourselves tomorrow.

Let me give you an example of how to use Dharma to transform your life. I had a lot of difficult, horrible experiences as a child, both physically and mentally. I suffered lots of physical and mental abuse.

My foster parents were very much against me practising Buddhism. They threatened to make me go to college and get married because it was their way. They had even already chosen a girl for me to marry! They wanted so much for me to go to college and not to pursue Dharma. They even resorted to saying nasty things about my Dharma teacher. They would spread rumors about him, saying he was having sex with all the women in the neighborhood. Some people believed them but 90 percent of them did not—it didn't matter and I didn't care.

If I had cared, and if my parents had been successful in stopping me from practicing the Dharma, we would not be here today and they would have collected incredible, negative karma. If I was to become a Dharma teacher and touch a thousand people in my life, they would have stopped me from touching those people. When someone has a real and genuine desire to do Dharma and we stop them, it is incredible, negative karma.

I resisted and fought. I ran away from my foster parents a lot, and I hurt them tremendously because I wanted to practice Dharma. I did not run away to hurt them but I had to find the courage to do it anyway because I knew what I needed to do.

Despite all that they did to prevent me from practising the Dharma, I still respect and pray for them, and make offerings for them because I know that how they acted was all they knew and that was their level of practice.

I choose not to use those experiences to create a further reputation for myself. I choose not to take the anger out on myself or others. What I choose to do is to realize that I did something in a previous life to get that experience. Therefore, I accept it.

By accepting, letting go and forgiving, I purify that karma. It is done. That karma is used up. I cannot use it any more. It is like a paper cup or a paper plate—once I have used it, it won't be used by another person again. However, if I harp on about it, if I focus on it and do negative things as a result of it, or if I justify my actions by saying that they are the result of being hurt and abused, I will be like the boy who cried wolf—in the end, no one will accept my justifications anymore. People may accept the justifications once or twice but not on a continual basis.

People who do not wish to find the courage to do something more, or take any action or responsibility, will justify their actions by bringing up previous experiences or things that were done to them in the past. They might say things like, "My husband was bad to me, my wife cheated on me, my mother was bad to me and my father was a womanizer." They continuously use their previous experiences as an excuse for their state of being now.

You may have had a horrible spouse in the past who cheated on you and lied to you. Or you may have had terrible parents who abused and beat you, and you did not get an education so you had a difficult time growing up. Yes, that is what happened and on a worldly level, we cannot deny it.

I am not saying that those past experiences have nothing to do with your state of being now. They may be contributing factors but you need to examine what is contributing to your downfall r*ight now*. What is contributing to your lack of knowledge and your justifications *right now? What is it that you are doing now?* Think about it logically—if those previous experiences have led to what you are now, your experiences now and today can lead to what you will be tomorrow.

You cannot live the rest of your life based on what has happened to you and continuously use that as a justification. That is you grasping and holding on to a projection, and not letting go of something that happened to you in the past. Instead, you will continue to create karma from that event. If you were at fault for what happened in the past, you reinforce that fault now by not letting go, and you will repeat it again and again with new people you meet. If you were not at fault, you are creating the fault now because when you hold on to the previous experience and you act out of it, you create more karma to have it happen again.

For example, I might have had an older brother who was very mean to me when I was young. For years, he would beat me up, and take my food and toys away. When I grow up and become a successful businessman, I get my revenge on him. He may be working in a low-paid job, struggling financially, and when he comes to ask for money, I make him kowtow to me and I make him feel small. I extract my revenge. What I should realize is that what he did to me is over but because I am holding on to past experiences, I act negatively towards him. From that past experience, I continue to create more and more and more negative karma.

How we live now is the result of our experiences or dreams, what we wanted to be or do, or the hopes we had earlier in life (or even in a previous life). Although it is sometimes hard to understand, we should let go and know that those experiences and dreams do not affect us anymore. Change now. Changing in Dharma, with Dharma, by Dharma creates new attitudes to experiences now and in the future. We transform so we do not create or sustain a negative reputation for ourselves, nor reaffirm our negative actions.

Thus, if we are creating negative karma now, it is due to our past experiences. We can examine that statement further— if we are creating a lot of negative karma now, it is due to the *reactions* we have had to our previous experiences. Think: people can be beaten and react positively. People can be beaten and react negatively.

Deep Dharma practitioners move on when they have been beaten. They say, "I have purified my karma. It is okay and I will avoid holding on to that in the future. I forgive the person," and from there, they do not create any more harm. People who do not move on will probably try and obtain revenge—they might become angry; they might even beat up or kill other people. Whatever it is, they will definitely hurt others by not moving on.

I do not deny that what happens to us now is based on our past experiences. However, if we keep basing what we do now—or tomorrow, the next day, the next week, the next year—on what has happened in the past, we will continue to live the way we are and never progress. In my case, if my parents had stopped me from learning and teaching the Dharma and benefiting people, I might have held on to that and be living now with a lot of anger and resentment.

When we base our current actions on previous experiences, things may even worsen for us because there will come a time when our age starts to show, when our metabolism slows down, and when the energy and zest of our youth goes away. Even if we still have the energy and zest of youth, it is not very significant either—many youths waste their time on activities that eventually destroy them emotionally.

When we hold on to our past experiences and base our current experiences on these past experiences, we lose on a worldly level. On a spiritual level, Buddhism explains that when we hold on like this, every prayer we say with the aspiration of benefiting all sentient beings becomes a farce and a lie, and we are fooling ourselves. If we cannot help ourselves to let go of something that happened in the past—which we may have created ourselves—then how can we help others?

Remember that I do not deny that the experience is there or that it happened. What I deny is how we *reacted* to the experience, and what we do in conjunction with and as a result of that experience. I am not simply talking about how we may have reacted immediately to that experience but also how we acted and held on to it the next year, and the next year, and the next year, all the way up until this moment.

Therefore, what has happened to us in the past is what we are now. Our past experiences have influenced our actions and the harm we are creating now. Following on from that logic, what will happen to us in the future depends on what we do *now*.

18 PEACE IS TRANSFORMING...

... Your Fate (Or What You Do When Your Luck Runs Out)

Enjoy what you have now. At the same time, however, you must work for your future.

However beautiful you are, you will not be beautiful one day. However young and healthy you are, you will not be young and healthy one day. However rich you are, your wealth will be taken away one day—you might lose it all while you are alive and you will definitely lose it all at the time of death. However many children you have, they will leave the flock one day. It is wonderful if you have set them on the right path; if you have not set them on the right path, it becomes a gamble whether they will make it in life or not. Ultimately, you have to let go.

If you have wonderful parents who take care of you and give you money, love, cars, food, a house, and everything else that you want, realize that they will be gone one day. Do not think that when they are gone you will have a big inheritance because if you do not have the merit to receive it, your parents will take their luck with them when they pass away and you will not receive that inheritance. When their luck is gone, you will not have that luck anymore. You will go down.

I have seen a lot of children who have experienced this. Throughout my life, I have met and talked with thousands of people, from all levels and cultures. I have met many children who were from extremely wealthy families but once their parents were gone, they fell. I am not putting anyone down. I am trying to explain that when some people do not have the luck themselves but live with someone who does, a little of that luck rubs off onto them.

For example, if you have bad body odour but you are standing next to someone who smells good, other people who come near the both of you will think that you both smell very good. However, when that nice-smelling person goes away and people can smell *you*, their reaction to what they smell will change—they will realize that you don't smell that good after all!

Similarly, if your parents are very wealthy, everyone will look at your family and think that you are all so lucky and rich, and have everything you need. However, once your parents die, you may suddenly become "smelly." If you do not have the luck to receive the wealth, you will not get a dime. I promise you! Something may go wrong in the courts or your relatives may fight for a share. Something will go wrong and you will not receive anything.

The same law of karma applies to everything in life. You may be standing next to a very powerful person who "smells" good but your own bad "smell" will come out once they are gone because you live by *your* karma, not theirs.

You need to change yourself so you no longer "smell bad," and the way to bring about that change is to listen to the Dharma, and to contemplate and practice what you learn. Even what I am telling you now is Dharma. Those of you who take the time to read a Dharma book will end up with more knowledge on how change yourself. When you finish reading these teachings, you will have done something for yourself—you will have gained knowledge with an incredible lineage, directly from Lord Buddha himself. You win. If you make the effort, stay awake, pay attention and read, you win.

According to His Eminence Kensur Jampa Yeshe Rinpoche, that way of living—of depending on the wealth of our parents, family or loved ones—is a speedy way of burning up our merit and creating the causes for not having anything later. For example, I may live with my father who takes care of everything for me. I can react to his kindness in two ways: First, I can choose not to take responsibility for myself in any way, shape or form; I just live the good life without making the most of it to do something better. My father is sheltering me now and giving me everything I want but if I do not take care of myself, I will fall when his shelter is gone.

Or, in response to my father's kindness, I can educate myself, improve myself, work harder and establish myself, even if I am being taken care of. I can choose to do something with my life. I am still being sheltered but I make sure that when my parents are gone, I am able to make it on my own merits, spiritually and materially.

What Kensur Jampa Yeshe Rinpoche refers to is the first type of person who does not use his good life to improve himself but uses up his merit faster. When this umbrella or shelter of this parent is gone, he will fall even harder.

I have seen this happen in my own family, among my half-brothers. One of them died of cancer when he was only in his early 40s. My birth father, who lives in Taiwan, is a very wealthy man. I do not get anything from him because I am from a different mother but my half-brothers were able to receive some of his wealth.[1]

One of them received several apartments and houses from my father but he died of cancer, perhaps because he drank too much, smoked too much and partied too much. He never worked a day in his life, as he lived off the money he received from renting out the apartments my father gave him. My brother literally died from a good life.

My sister took some land from my father and sold it. She received three to four million dollars from the sale then disappeared to another part of Taiwan and never contacted him again. My other brother is now living under the umbrella of my father.

My point is that my father will go one day. He has throat cancer and although he is well now because it is in remission, he will have to go one day. When the security of my father's umbrella is gone, my siblings will suffer tremendously. When we live under someone else's luck and merits, no matter how close they are to us, we may not get their wealth when they are gone. What adds to the sadness is that the people and friends who are around us now will disappear very quickly when that person and that wealth we are living off from is gone. That is what happened to my half-brothers.

I am not telling you all this from a Dharma book or from something I read. I am talking from my own experience and it matches what the Buddha has taught. That is just a small glimpse into my family background. Do not think that I have had a good life, that I received money from my birth father and have been living in a golden palanquin in the Potala Palace. No! I did not have the fortune to receive that wealth from my father; I did not have the good life.

I am not trying to scare you, and make your life all doom and gloom. If you are going to live and be the way you are now, please enjoy what you have. At the same time, however, you must work for your future, whether you want to do it based on Dharma and karma, or from a basis of self-preservation— *just do it*. Do it because what you have now is based on the past, but the past cannot always become the future—the way you are living now means you are using up your merits very quickly, and you will not have the merits to sustain the same lifestyle in the future.

PART V

Peace Is Not About...

19 PEACE IS NOT ABOUT...

...Love and Hatred

Our perception of a person or an object can change so fast. It is proof that our perception is the enemy.

When we love, like, hate or dislike an object, a person, a living being or a non-living object, that is not reality. When we like something, it is not based on a true, realistic view of the object. If it is—and you can check it, based on a true, realistic study of the object we are attached to or like—then our attachment to or liking of the object or person must be permanent. But if that person says something to us that we don't like, we may start to dislike them. Yesterday, we could have been the best of friends, and we praised them from here to high heaven; tomorrow, we could absolutely dislike them.

At the same time, the object that we like can be disliked by other people; and the object that we dislike can be liked by other people. Therefore, the object itself doesn't have an inherent or intrinsic nature to be liked or disliked. It is our afflicted perception that sees an object and says, "we like" or "we don't like."

When we see an object and we like it, we build on it. When we see a beautiful girl, we think that since she's beautiful, she's going to stay beautiful, that there's no way she will get fat, old, sick or lose her beauty. We also think that she will have a beautiful family, a wonderful job and a great, clean house. Everything about her is going to be fabulous because *she is beautiful*.

We have this afflictive perception of the object and are attracted to it. When we meet reality, we think, "Why is she like that? How can she talk or act like that?" We always ask why things are like that. It is because they *are* like that but we had thought that they were otherwise.

When we dislike something or when someone says something to us that we don't like, we automatically start to dislike that person. They might have had a bad day or a problem at the time, and said something unpleasant to us. Instantly, our afflicted perceptions build upon what they said to us. We think, "Since they're rude to me, they're also ugly. They probably eat unhealthy foods, they've probably got diseases and they probably don't have any friends. They probably have bad businesses, they have ugly, mean parents, they have nasty siblings and even their dog has rabies."

But the minute we hear that perhaps that person's mother has had a car accident, and is now in a serious condition in the hospital, our perception changes immediately. We start to feel sorry for that person. Our perception of a person or an object can change so fast. It is proof that our perception is the enemy. We perceive wrongly. Perception is to see, hear, feel, touch, taste and smell; to perceive wrongly is afflicted because it *brings about affliction* and there is something wrong with it. Affliction is a disease, something that makes you suffer or makes you unwell. Mental affliction arises from the same cause as the result. Therefore, mental affliction arises from distorted mental perception.

Change yourself by realizing that all perception is afflicted. Since it is afflicted, it can be changed, and since it can be changed, you will get the opposite result if you change it. Don't complain you're lonely. If you complain that you're lonely to anybody in this room, they're going to tell you, "You have A.E.! Afflictive Emotion."

Think about it. You've got A.E. syndrome, I've got A.E. syndrome, and we're all talking about it. "Hi, my name is Tsem Rinpoche, I'm 44, and I'm suffering from A.E." This is what it's all about—afflictive emotions! It sounds funny, but it's true.

When you operate on that basis where you don't know that very simple yet profound truth, you will go through life making enemy after enemy after enemy. When you follow a wrong perception, whether it's positive or negative, it will disappoint you. If you are in a wonderful relationship, it is going to be *not* wonderful. Your husband turns out to be an absolute, boring nightmare. He's different from you, and only interested in karaokes, card games and wet t-shirt contests. Your wife turns out to be an absolute nightmare too. She's got really smelly breath and armpits; she just really took care of herself on the day you got married. And she's got a horrible mother who nags you to death: "Why are you not a dentist? Why are you not a doctor? Why is my daughter still driving around in a BMW from last year?"

The problems just go on and on and on. All these things come out. All of a sudden, one misunderstanding after another arises, and you decide to separate. When you separate, you go to court. You say they're wrong, they say you're wrong. It doesn't end.

Then you find the next person, and the next, and the next. After awhile, you settle down. Not because you have found the perfect person but because you have settled for less and you realize that there is no perfect person. Those of us who are smart stick with the person we are with and we just deal with it. There is no perfect person.

Even our perception of unhappiness is afflicted. Some of us are unhappy because we don't have a lover or a partner. We become depressed because of that, and we focus everything on that. People like that who get a partner will suffer even more than normal people because their perception of what makes them happy was wrong from the start! Some of us have horrible relationships that we would like to get out of.

If you are attached to a person or an object—such as money, a house, position, fame or reputation—and you hold on to it, it is your wrong afflicted perception that the respective person or object will give you happiness. In fact, those people or objects create more unhappiness and more problems.

For example, money makes you more wary, it doesn't let you open up to people, it makes you become stingy and protective; you spend all your time and energy making sure no one takes that money away from you. Every day you have that money, you think you're secure, but actually your security dwindles away more and more. That money eats away at you until you're an older, insecure, scared, fragile person. People who have had plenty of money for a long time live in total fear of what will happen if they don't have it anymore. Even while they have money, they can't enjoy it, although outwardly it looks like they do.

You can apply that to anything else that people think they love, like a house or a car. The minute you take that house or that car away, or something happens to it and they don't have it anymore, they suffer tremendously. They can go into depression, even suicide. Suffering of this type arises from wrong afflicted perception.

When you operate on a basis of afflicted perception, you will have a lot of unhappiness. You don't need to see into people's minds to know them. You look at their actions, how they talk and speak, what they focus and dwell on, and you will understand the level of their mind.

There are people who talk about "Me, myself and I" all the time. They complain, "*I'm* not happy, *I* didn't get what I want, *I* was disturbed, people did this to *me*, *I* did this and this is what they did to *me*." They only ever tell you what everyone has done to them that is wrong: *everyone* is an enemy, *everyone* is at fault, *everyone* is wrong. They believe that only their perception is correct.

These people are usually unhappy, because they refuse to take responsibility and they continuously blame others. They blame others because they have strong afflicted perception and they build on that, rather than on the truth.

If you do a simple meditation, think about that and reinforce that in your mind every day, you will see your wrong perception lessen. Enemies become friends, friends become neutral. In fact, everyone becomes neutral.

...Monsters and Angels

All monsters are wrongly afflicted perceptions. And so are all angels.

Having special attachment to and love for family members is not compassion. That type of love is not love. That is distorted love that comes from attachment. Attachment means to be connected to something or to attach yourself to someone without truth, reasoning or logic.

After a while, you will realize that your love for your husband, wife, friends, parents, loved ones and the people who have been kind to you is dependent on many factors—how they treat you, your mood or what is happening in your life at the time.

If we have a special love for our husband or our wife, it is because of and totally dependent on what the person does for us, and how he or she makes us feel. If they do things for us, then we love them; if they continue doing things for us, we continue to love them. If they stop, we don't love them anymore. The most precious people in our lives—like our parents—can become our worst enemies. There are people who never speak to their parents. There are people who can be the worst enemies with a person one day and best friends the next.

We may start by loving our husband and our children. That is the beginning of developing true compassion, but we should not stop there. We should not run around saying, "I'm good to my kids, my mother, my father, my husband and my friends." Yes, you *are* good to them; and if they were kind to you and you return their kindness, that is a very good human quality to start with. But that's just a normal quality. It's nothing special to develop and nothing to brag about.

Even animals will follow you, guard you loyally and have the capacity to feel love and attention for you when you feed them, pet them and speak nice words. However, their intelligence level is very low, so that is all they can perceive. Their love and loyalty to you is unchanging because their perception is limited.

If we operate on a level where we "love" only our mother, father and children, that is not compassion. It is afflicted emotion. We love our mother because she did something for us—she suckled us, took care of us, watched us, raised us and was the first symbol of kindness when she offered us her milk, the first symbol of compassion.

Having said that, according to Shantideva's *Bodhicharyavatara*,[1] we must start at that point, where we

172

focus on an ordinary level on the kindness of a being who has been kind to us. Then we expand outwards. We should not just love our mother and people who have been kind to us for the rest of our lives and not love anyone else. Then we cannot develop universal compassion because this love is based on distorted views. At the moment, we love a person not out of altruistic compassion or because we wish to relieve their problems and suffering. We "love them" because they have done something for us.

We start there but we don't end there. We can't spend the rest of our lives just loving our wives, husbands, children and people who are close to us. Since that type of emotion is afflicted—we love them only because they have done something for us—then our level remains that of an animal.

In fact, just loving our partners, friends and people who are good to us, collects negative karma and we reinforce the self-cherishing mind; we reinforce this mind that can love passionately and hate passionately. The actions that arise from that type of love and hatred will create the causes for us to take rebirth again and again in states of existence where we have even less opportunity to practice and realize the truth behind what creates our unhappiness.

The secret here is not to hate your wife, and not to hate everybody around you; the secret here is also not to love your wife, and not to love everybody around you. The secret here is to accept the people around you and the people you see *as they are*, not what you have mentally made them into—as monsters or angels. All monsters are wrongly afflicted perceptions. And so are all angels.

Even the most hardened criminals love someone—it could be their wife, mother or sister. Even the meanest person in the world does something kind for someone they are attached to. For example, even if everyone in this room was my enemy and I hated all of you, my opinion could change overnight if all of you grouped together and decided to help me, to give me whatever I needed, talked to me and said something that I liked.

So, even while we hate a few people, it is not true hatred and it is not reality. The minute the causes or the conditions change for that hatred, our hatred changes. We have experienced that many times.

Afflicted love and care, and afflicted hatred and dislike are two sides of the same coin because they arise from wrong perception of the object. It is not the object arising as good or bad, friend or enemy, black or white, positive or negative—it is our wrong perception of that being. A person who has realized that will not have any more "enemies." He will also not have any more "friends." He will have taken the first step towards developing compassion. He will enter the *Bodhisattva* level.

When you let go of like and dislike based on a meditation of destroying afflicted perception, you will enter the *Bodhisattva* practice. Then, you will not hate anyone and you will abide in reality. Reality is compassion. Realism is compassion. This compassion, this ability to love others regardless of what they do to you, is your true nature.

If you have hated someone for a very long time—a brother, sister, a wife or a husband—let it go because it is just your perception. Every single day that you hate a person (or every day that you love a person out of afflicted desire), you create even more causes to take rebirth in *samsara*.

Loving something intensely and hating something intensely collects very negative karma. Loving something intensely increases our attachment—afflicted attachment. Hating something intensely increases the habituation of dwelling in non-realistic perception.

Therefore, it behooves us *not* to hate, *not* to confront, *not* to fight back, *not* to shout, *not* to yell and *not* to be revengeful. It is very important not to engage in these actions because temporarily, we create unhappiness for ourselves and others; ultimately, we reinforce this mind to do it more and more and more, until it becomes completely natural and habitual, and we become a total nightmare on legs. Wherever we go, we will create unhappiness; whatever we do, we will be unhappy. Even our physical body—our facial expressions and our body language—will create displeasure in other people's minds. We will allow our habituation to grow because we practice and engage in the wrong perception that makes us think everyone is an enemy.

To hate or like someone is not reality because it is based on afflicted emotion. Afflicted emotions do not focus on reality nor how the object that we perceive really exists. It "exists" based on how we perceive it. Therefore, it is false and brings us unhappiness. Therefore, universal hatred is impossible: it is based on wrong perception and wrong view; it is not reality nor is it the truth. It depends not only on the object but also on the viewer.

Universal hatred is not possible; permanent hatred is not possible. Universal hatred, anger and disgust of people and things are not natural, not permanent and not your real state of mind. That is why when you engage in it, you never experience happiness. This is because what you are suffering arises from afflicted wrong view. Therefore, when it is removed, only right view can exist, and when right view exists, the result will be compassion and forgiveness.

On the other hand, universal compassion is possible, because compassion is based on reality, while hatred is based on non-reality. Compassion and forgiveness is your natural state of mind. Universal compassion is the direction you need to head towards and once you develop it, it is permanent.

It is like if you want to sharpen metal into a sword, you have to have the metal first. If you don't have the metal, what will you be sharpening? In the same way, you have intrinsically in you the true nature of Buddhahood—compassion. If you work on it by meditating on what I have explained, you can develop that mental state. It is possible and it is your reality: compassion is reality.

...Extreme Fear or Extreme Happiness

Being attached to outer things is just a symptom; the real attachment is to ourselves.

When you have extreme fear, you will also have extreme happiness. When you have extreme happiness, you will also have extreme fear—they are two sides of the same coin.

For example, when you get a gift, when someone compliments you, when you're going on a trip, when you get some food that you like, go shopping or watch a movie, you might become extremely happy. You might jump up and down, and scream. You would sacrifice everything—yourself, your friends, the people around you, your purpose, your job or your commitments—to be happy. You become irresponsible. And yet, you are very, very "happy."

It is fine if you are jumping up and down and screaming for comedic reasons because it is entertaining but if you really feel like that deep down inside, it is actually a very bad sign.

When you are happy about shopping, getting gifts, meeting someone or doing something, it is not a normal happiness. It is a kind of happiness where you are so excited deep down inside that you would sacrifice everything for it. That kind of happiness is very dangerous—for us, for others and for everyone in the long term.

This is because we have a very strong conceptual projection that outer items create our happiness. We have a very strong projection that, "If I have reputation, if I have gifts, if I have material things, if I have this person, if I have this situation and if I go here, *I will be very happy.*"

When we think like that, we become very depressed and very unhappy. We are not able to function to our full potential because we keep holding on to outer circumstances, outer phenomenon and material objects to make us happy. When those items are taken away or when our wishes are not fulfilled, we become very unhappy, very depressed, very sad or very angry.

If those items brought us happiness and were the real cause of us being happy, then the more we have, the happier we should become. And if those items were the real cause of our happiness, then our level of happiness should not revert backwards if they were taken away; we should still remain happy.

For example, when we develop qualities in meditation, in Dharma or in compassion, we remain at that level of happiness even if the object that helped us to develop those qualities is taken away. For example, if our Guru dies, the level of happiness we attained in our practice will remain. Lord Buddha's Guru died but Lord Buddha still attained Enlightenment. It didn't take away from his Enlightenment. All the Gurus of masters like Lama Tsongkhapa and Milarepa died and their caves were taken away. When you hear the stories of a lot of great masters, you will learn about the tremendous difficulties they had to go through and the things they had to sacrifice but you don't see any them being bitter. They are sad, but they are not bitter or unhappy. And they are not faking it.

In some cases (though not in all, as it depends on our karma and situation), if we have a relationship, we become happier and happier and happier, one year, after another, after another. In eighty to eighty-five per cent of cases, this is not what happens.

You might ask why people live together their whole lives. It is not that they are happy living together. They are unhappy but they have become used to it, they are not as good-looking or fresh anymore, and it is not easy to start all over again. When they are very old and have no one to depend on, when they are used to the person, when they know what is good or bad about them and they can deal with it, they stay with each other. They call that happiness, they say they are happy and they love that person. (I have seen a few exceptional cases, of course.)

Look at ourselves and the clothes we wear. How excited are we when we get new clothes? And after a while, how do we feel? It is the same when we get a new piece of jewelry, when we go on a trip or when we meet a new friend. When some people meet someone new and feel that this could be "the one," their excitement is very obvious. After a few weeks, they become disgusted. Their projection was that this person would be everything they thought he or she would be.

Look at us with inanimate objects and animate beings, both of which bring us unhappiness. If inanimate objects bring us happiness, we are the type of person that needs to be entertained, to find excitement and material things—like jewelry, clothes and cars—to jolt our brains. We get bored after a while. When we see new things, we become even more bored with what we have and we think, "If I have this instead, I will be happier." Why do you think the advertising world makes billions of dollars? They play on this projection. That's all it is.

As for animate beings—such as pets, people, parties and discos—we go to these places and meet these people with a projection. We think, "I look good, I'm going to go there and I'm going to attract." If, for some reason, we don't attract, we don't get what we want, we're not the center of attention, or the people we attract are not what we like, we go home very depressed. We feel that all the preparation has been wasted. Most of us prepare a week ahead if we want to go out. We go on a diet, get a haircut and go for facials. Then, when we go to these places and we don't find or attract what we want, all this effort falls flat on our faces and we become depressed.

These people who are very excited about what they have are prone to depression, anxiety attacks, fear and not want-ing to do more because they are afraid to lose. These types of people are actually extroverted introverts: they look very happy and outgoing but if you put them in a situation within a group where they have to perform or be themselves, they cannot handle it.

It is not that they are bad people. It is because they have been disappointed by many things in the past. However, they have to understand that the disappointment does not come from something on the outside. It comes from their own projection that they would be happy *if only* they had these things.

Being attached to these outer things—people and items—is just a symptom; the real attachment is to ourselves. People who are very excited and jump up and down very excitedly about getting new things and material items, going to new places or meeting new people are actually very selfish people.

A lot of these people blame their depression on everyone and everything else on the outside. When these people fall, they go into the deepest depression; they get depressed at the drop of a hat. The rougher ones get very angry and can become violent, beat up their wives, run out and scream at people, become twisted, trick people and lie. They vent their anger on the whole world, at everybody around them. Then, these emotions of anger, trickery and deception grow; when this anger grows, it becomes a habit and they become very angry people. They will become angry at anything and everything.

Within the same type of mind, a person can also be very subtle about his excitement. He may not jump up and down about receiving something, or become overtly depressed and angry about not receiving something. However, this type of person is still very attached to what he has or what he should have, and he finds a sense of security, happiness and well-being only if he has these things. These people are very quiet and secretive about everything having to do with them: their personal life, job, plans, love life and finances. They project an aura of simplicity, renunciation and non-attachment. But when you know them better and examine their mind, it is very different.

It doesn't matter if the quiet types don't jump up and down when they receive something. These people go into very deep anxiety attacks instead. Extreme cases lead to suicide. Actually, these people suffer much more than the first type because they hide their suffering. Suffering is suffering. Their attachment to themselves is as strong as everybody else's; it is just their manifestation of it that is different. It does not mean that someone's suffering is less intense just because he is quiet about it.

These people who expend a lot of energy hiding, masking and covering are very extreme because they expend more energy hiding their attachment. They are more likely to suffer, commit suicide or go insane. I have met many people like that and the most predominant are people who have money.

Those people come in four categories. First, there are the ones who flaunt their wealth but do not want to share. Second, they flaunt their wealth and they do share. The third type does not flaunt their wealth at all and does not share. The last type does not flaunt their wealth but does share. All are very attached to their money.

I have met a lot of people who have lost 30 to 60 million dollars. They have every right to be depressed and unhappy! But they are the same people who always tell you they don't have anything and are very stingy to help, share or give. I have met very beautiful, educated, sophisticated ladies who are really dressed to impress. When they come for a divination,[1] it is revealed that they have lost astronomical amounts of money. When they come into the room, when the door is closed and they are alone, they begin to cry. They are shaking but they keep it very quiet because they do not want people to know.

Observe these people who get very excited about things. They should observe themselves: how depressed and unhappy they become. They will be very erratic, inconsistent, and very, very sketchy and unreliable in anything they do because of their depression and fear. The depression arises from disappointment; fear arises from more depression. They will be unstable—their moods, relationships and commitments will all be unstable. They will only do the bare minimum that they have to do to survive.

These people—as they wallow and think about themselves over and over again—never improve. They go through a lifetime of forgetfulness, lack of awareness, lack of commitment, not achieving anything, not moving on or doing anything. It would still be okay if they did not commit to or achieve anything on the outside, but they have to have achieved something on the *inside*.

22 PEACE IS NOT ABOUT...

... Living in Paradise

Our perception of a person or an object can change so fast. It is proof that our perception is the enemy.

Whether you are attached to someone you love totally, or you are attached to someone you hate totally, both states of mind bring you down to the three lower realms.

Don't be attached to your children. Don't be attached to your husband. Don't be attached to your cousin. Don't be attached to your mother. Don't be attached to your lover, your wife or your house. Don't be. You can have all that, but have it with compassion. Then by living this way every day, you will not create the causes for you to suffer.

The ones with the biggest position, the biggest name and the most wealth will suffer the most because everything reinforces their fears and their non-perception of reality. The secret here is not to give up money, position, your wife, your husband or your children—the secret here is to do what you need to do for them but to realize that you are only here for a short time. If you keep existing for the sake of only making yourself happy based on external objects, you will *not* be happy because those are not the causes of happiness. If you have experienced any "happiness" from these external objects, it is false, it is made up, it is you telling yourself you are happy. Actually, you are not.

We look at a lot of people and think they must be very happy because they have a husband, a wife, or this and that. Why do you think those gossip magazines are so popular, so powerful and make billions of dollars? Because they tell us the truth: the stars and their beautiful husbands and wives are *not* happy! There's trouble in paradise. (It's very important "Dharma" for me to find out they're not happy too because I keep wanting to be them!)

Why do you think stars get divorced so frequently? Because they have everything to accelerate their unhappiness. They have too much money, too much praise, too much fame, too much beauty, too much of everything. That is why whatever happens to us happens to them more and quicker because it accelerates their wrong view of what makes them happy.

Therefore, whether you are attached to someone you love totally, or you are attached to someone you hate totally, both states of mind bring you down to the three lower realms. You don't even have to go to the three lower realms[1]—when you live like that, you are in the three lower realms now because you are always in a state of mental anguish.

Some of you have a relationship and some of you don't, but please trust me when I tell you that it is exactly the same. Some of you are as poor as church mice and some of you are as rich as Dzambala but your suffering and your experiences are the same. And you are likely to end up going to the same place. Think about that. I'm not lying, I'm not making it up and I'm not trying to make sweeping, generalised statements. Think about it based on what I have just said.

Some people want a relationship or want to keep a relationship but wanting it so badly will create the causes not to have it. If we search within ourselves, it could be a physical problem, a disciplinary problem or an emotional problem that has resulted in us not having a relationship and feeling lonely—it could be all of that. Whatever it is, it is not permanent because all those reasons have causes and conditions that can be changed, removed and replaced.

If any of those causes and conditions are changed, removed and replaced, and *we* change, we would be able to get a relationship. We might not get a shining prince on a beautiful, big, white horse with a big bag of gold; but perhaps a nice, little, bald guy in a Volkswagen comes along and keeps us company instead. We might not get a beautiful fairy princess who wakes up when we kiss her, who's fabulous and lets us drink champagne out of her shoes; but perhaps we get a girl who's a little heavy, and we wouldn't want to even sniff her sneakers, but she's sweet and we're not lonely. For some of us, that's fine.

Change the causes and conditions, and you will then attract what you want, though it may not be exactly what was in your fantasies, dreams and videos, or what you've been wanting and bragging to your friends about.

You say, "But you just talked about not having attachment." Yes, but you *are* attached, so deal with it! After reading this, you don't go from first level *Bodhisattvahood* to third level, become unattached and see Buddhas. You still want a relationship, food, love, *boobali* and money. It's not going to be instant so you need something to help you along the way. If you've got a headache and it's coming from something serious like a viral infection, don't say you won't take Aspirin because that's not going to heal the cause of the problem. Don't be stupid! Take the Aspirin *and* take the antibiotics!

Along the way to healing, you need something to help you. Along the path to non-attachment, have something to tide you over. That's not bad but you must also realize what is the truth and what is happening—then you won't suffer as much and you won't create more negative karma.

If you want a relationship, realize that what you have been doing for yourself and the things which you are supposed to do but are not doing, are based on your wrong perception. Switch it. If you are having problems in your relationship, those problems are based on your wrong perception. Switch it. Do not be narrow-minded.

23 PEACE IS NOT ABOUT...

...Clinging on to Attachments

There is a huge difference between having something to live and using it to benefit others, and hoarding it and saying that you are happy because you have it.

We have to think about the things that supposedly bring us happiness—such as wealth, beauty, friends, possessions, shopping, movies, fun, music, dancing, singing, clothes, ornaments, real estate or travelling—because we have to look at how unhappy we really are.

We have to look at whether those things, or living in those ways, have helped us to expand in life, get us further into betterment. If the answer is no, we have to look at the symptoms and results. The symptoms for every single sentient being on this planet, in varying degrees, is not finishing what we start, and a lack of commitment and awareness.

On an inner level, we suffer a lot of depression, which is a sense of defeat and hopelessness. The depression increases and eventually, we use that as an excuse for not accomplishing anything. We say that we are depressed. Most people will have sympathy for us if we say that we are depressed because they think we have done our best and we are just feeling down. What they do not understand is that for people who are depressed all the time, it is not actually depression anymore; it is just a way to hide from doing things. I know that because I was depressed many times, for many, many years. Then I looked deeper, and I knew what it really was that made me feel that way.

We will also have a lot of anger. Anything will tick us off, make us unhappy, angry and frustrated. *Anything.* This is because we're grasping onto external things that we think make us happy, instead of moving away from them or becoming stronger and stronger. Then we let the anger turn to bitterness, a sense that everything is wrong, everything will be wrong and will remain wrong.

That bitterness and what we see around us is "correct." People *do* disappoint, things *do* disappoint and opportunities *do* disappoint. But for us to be bitter about everything around us that causes us disappointment is a wrong view. Everything you see in people is disappointing. It is. But for people who do not grasp onto permanence and projections, seeing the disappointments around them will push them to work harder in response to the disappointments.

For example, we might look at a practitioner who we thought was fabulous. After living and hanging out with them for a year or two, we discover they are not fabulous. We might become bitter and angry; then we do not want to associate with them anymore and we cut them off. That is a sign of a person who has very strong grasping. In fact, in response to this, we should work harder for them. If working harder for them at this moment is not beneficial, then we should work harder on ourselves so that when we encounter more and more of these types of people, we can work in response to them.

We will meet more and more of these people: *everyone* in *samsara* will disappoint us. There is not one person in our lives who has not disappointed us—from our teachers and Gurus, to our best friends, to people on the street. Think about it. Everyone disappoints you. Do you know why everyone disappoints you? Because you are hanging on to a projection, you are hanging on to how they *should be* and how *you* should be treated. You are not thinking about them, you are not thinking about others. You are thinking about yourself. That is why you become depressed.

Having something and the motive behind having it are two very different things. There is a huge difference between having something to live and using it to benefit others, and hoarding it and saying that you are happy because you have it. The karma that is created is different, so when the karma ripens, the result will also be different. The whole reason and mode of having that thing is different.

All of us in *samsara* are the same. How we manifest our *samsara* is different but for all of us, this comes from thinking that external items are the cause of our happiness and not realising that we suffer when these external items are taken away. That comes from not believing in or understanding impermanence.

Lord Buddha says that all things that are born and live must die. We must understand that fundamental truth. When we meditate on this in detail with examples, over and over again, we will see that our attachment to a lot of things on the outside becomes less.

When you tell people that they can't be attached and they can't have the things they want, they will start to have very big fears. A lot of Westerners experience a lot of fear because they are not from a culture where frugality, simplicity or hiding wealth is a virtue. There, you have to flaunt it. Look at all the pop singers' music videos on television! They flaunt everything they have. In the West, they tell you directly, "Isn't it fabulous? My house is fabulous, my food is fabulous, *I'm* fabulous." If you don't agree, they freak out and they ask, "Why *not*?" It is not much better in the East. There, they hide everything they have. In the East, you have to be more deceptive: "I don't have anything, my food's not good, my house is not good," but they expect you to say something else—that it *is* good and it *is* wonderful. If you don't say that it's good, they freak out.

If you go for dinner at your aunt's house, you have to say, "Your dinner is delicious, Aunty!" Then, she would say, "No, no, it's not good. It's just something I threw together," even though she's been working on it for the whole week. But if you don't keep complimenting her profusely, she's going to be very upset! There is no difference between the East and the

West. It's just opposite extremes and different manifestations of *samsara*. There is no difference at all.

If you want happiness and contentment, if you want your mind to be calm and if you want to enjoy items that supposedly bring you suffering, you have to realize impermanence. Understand that anything and nothing—and being attached to it—can bring you unhappiness. If you understand and realize this, and you focus on it, you will start seeing your mind calm down. That is definite.

You need to understand that this does not mean you cannot have these things. It means that these things should not make you happy or unhappy. Look at examples of people like Mother Teresa, who received millions and millions of dollars in donations. People just wrote her million-dollar cheques and world-famous people came to meet her. It wasn't like that 30 or 40 years before she started her holy mission but she remained exactly the same when she started her mission, during her missionary work and towards the end. Getting material items and having people come to meet her didn't make her happy or unhappy, excited or depressed. I've read and seen many times in books and movies about her that when she received all these funds she would say immediately, "Oh, I know who I can give this to. I'm so happy!"

When she wanted a piece of land and couldn't get it, she would go from Calcutta to the Indian minister's office in Delhi. This diminutive, tiny, little lady would walk into the minister's office, sit in front of him and say, "I want this piece of land there." The minister would be very respectful because everyone knew who she was. He would say, "No, I can't give that to you, that's prime land, that's 70 acres you're asking for! And it's in Delhi!"

She would say, "No, I must have this for the lepers. What is the Government doing for the lepers? I don't mean any offence to you."

He said, "You know, our Government is not very rich and we're having problems."

She said, "That's why I want to do it. I'm not criticising the Government. I'm asking if I can please help these people. Because while you're having your meetings, these people are dying on the streets with no dignity. And they're spreading their disease. So let me help. Let me have that piece of land. What's the difference if you sold the land and got that money to give to them; or if you gave me the land and I raised the funds to give them dignity and jobs?"

The ministers went inside, talked, came out and said something like, "I'll give you 40 acres."

She said, very sincerely, "No, I want 70."

He said, "Please, great Mother. We'll give you 50."

She said, "70."

Finally, he said, "Okay. 70."

You must read this. You will cry. She's so "greedy" but no one gets offended or upset and they respect her for her "greed" because they know what it is for. When she doesn't get something, she's upset and unhappy because of the pain of not being able to achieve what she wanted to do with it.

People like that, who receive *millions* of dollars and who have a lot of respect, care and millions of people looking at them do not get affected by any of those external things because the reason for them getting those things is very different.

Mother Teresa did get depressed too. She was depressed and upset because she couldn't go over to Afghanistan to help when there was a war there and people were dying (she was not allowed to go because of political reasons). We're upset because we made it into a movie late and we missed 20 minutes; we get depressed and we scream at our friends. We're depressed because we have 10 million dollars in the bank and someone asked us to buy them dinner. That's what *we* get depressed and unhappy about!

You can't go through your whole life blaming everything, everyone and yourself for the things you don't have or couldn't do, and not achieve anything on the inside or outside. This is actually a result of your extreme grasping toward permanence, which does not exist.

When we meditate on that and we collect merits towards realizing that, I promise you it will become better and better and better. You will remain essentially the same. If you dress like a prostitute, you will continue dressing like a prostitute, but your whole reason for dressing—and doing all these other external things—will be different. You will still like food, going on trips, shopping, making and saving money. You will still like all of that and you will do everything as you did before but it will not create suffering and instead, will benefit others. In fact, by doing these things—getting angry, going shopping, keeping and making money—you will, in fact, collect merit. Your whole intention for doing these things will become different.

You will be like a vampire. When people get bitten by vampires, they become vampires themselves, but they remain essentially the same. If they were beautiful before, they will still be beautiful; if they liked wine, they will still like wine; if they liked music, they will still like music. Whatever they were before and whatever they are now as a vampire remains exactly the same. The only difference is that their reason to live and do things now has changed.

The secret here is not about having or not having something. The secret here is the *reason* for having it. And the reason you should have it is not just something intellectual. The reason or motivation for having it is based on understanding impermanence, understanding grasping and understanding why your mind becomes unhappy because of these things.

Then, you can have everything that you're comfortable with without getting upset if you don't have it, or if it is taken away from you. Whether you have these things or not will not make you happy or unhappy anymore. You will also be able to share what you have; and when you can share what you have, you will see your spiritual practice grow.

Then, you will see a fundamental difference. You will continue getting angry, but your anger will be used to benefit; it will not be used to harm. You will notice that when you get angry at people, and when other people get angry, one has result and one doesn't. Consider this example: when our mothers get angry at us, what results does her anger bring? We do what she wants, which are usually very good things because our mothers only want the best for us.

If you look at things that way and if you understand and realize this, you will become less depressed, you will get along with other people better, you will gain more courage to do things you're afraid of and you will definitely have less anxiety. You will be consistent, keep your commitments, be less angry and less emotional, and accept things more easily. Your bitterness will be greatly lessened, if not eradicated.

PART VI

Peace Gives Us...

24 PEACE GIVES US...

...Freedom to Let Go

As a result of holding on to our projections and expectations, we create more suffering for everyone.

We need to let go of conventions, projections, cultures, upbringing and expectations of experiences. When we do not project expectations onto others, we will not be disappointed when those expectations or projections are not met. By letting go of these expectations, we will feel less loss; and in feeling less loss, we will find purpose in our lives.

Let me give you an example. If we are Chinese, we might think that everything must be red during Chinese New Year. We might believe that if there is no red, we will not be prosperous in the coming year. This means that everyone who does not wear or have red during Chinese New Year will be a failure. We become attached to that thought.

I am not putting down Chinese culture and 5,000 years of rich Chinese heritage. What I mean to say is that if it suits everyone to have red, have red! If you go home to your family in your hometown and it makes them happy to use red everywhere, then you should use red everywhere. However, if you go somewhere else and a big argument ensues because you want red but the people there don't want red, it won't be a very happy *Gong Xi Fa Cai*,[1] will it?! By insisting on having red, you are trying to uphold a convention, which is something that is just created by humans who say we need to do things a certain way for good fortune to come to us.

Celebrate Chinese New Year with red if you want—wear red, have red houses and make everything red. Be red! However, if you are in a place that does not understand your tradition, you should realize that you do not have to hold yourself to that tradition, force it on to people and tell them that you *have* to have it. Holding on to culture and tradition can be beneficial but if we do it incorrectly, it can be harmful, even evil. It can hurt people.

Projections—how we expect a situation or a person to be—work in the same way. Most of us suffer because our projections are not fulfilled. We have a projection of how certain situations should be, how people should be and how we should do certain things. When the situation does not materialize as we have projected or when people do not act in a way we have expected, we become angry because our projections have not been fulfilled. Why have they not been fulfilled? Because, in the first place, our upbringing, culture, background and what we expected *were false*.

In holding on to our expectations, we also create suffering for other people. When we project false expectations onto others and they fail to "fulfill" those expectations, we might then scold them, become angry and moody, or say nasty things. As a result of holding on to our projections and expectations, we create more suffering for everyone.

It is okay if you do not believe in karma, religion and Buddha. But believe in humanity. Believe that you do not create harmony and happiness by your projections or when you project your expectations onto other people. You do not even need to believe in a next life to experience the benefits of letting go of your projections. Just believe in *this life*. Believe that if you project your own ideas onto others, it can only cause harm for everyone.

...Strength to Grow Up

For some people, the negative experience of living on the streets is a result of positive karma. It is something they prayed for.

It is actually a result of negative karma to have had a very easy life and everything given to you on a silver platter. People who have had parents who take care of them, give them money, nurture them, don't let them go through pain, learning or experience and don't let them grow, are suffering the result of extreme negative karma from previous lives. Why is that? Because they will take the wealth, leisure and opportunity to have a good time and use it frivolously; they won't care or will not be conscious about tomorrow or about other people; they will not be conscientious, will not push themselves or make an effort, and they will not experience their full potential. It is very good if they do have money for the rest of their lives but that money will bring them down to a lower and lower and lower level.

I know this because I have met many examples of people like this. These people cannot take responsibility, they are socially retarded, they are not able to perceive reality correctly, they are not able to put in effort, push themselves or achieve anything on their own. Everything must be given to them. If anything is taken away, they show a sour face, they suffer depression, anxiety and they start to think, "Poor me, I can't do it."

A sign of this attitude or tendency is their silence; they usually keep quiet because they are waiting for someone else to come up with a solution. This is because they draw from previous experiences, where they have always expected someone else to give them a solution. The same patterns of behavior repeat themselves as they become older.

As these people are growing up, their parents give them solutions to everything, and it is all cute and nice. Little Johnny and Little Diana are fine. But when Little Johnny and Little Diana grow up and come across a new situation where people cannot or will not give them the solutions, will not entertain their spoilt actions or help them, they will become depressed.

Previously, when they acted in a certain way, they received a certain response. Now, when they act in the same way, they receive a different response. When the previous response, the new response and their psyche do not match, depression, unhappiness and feelings of self-pity and hopelessness sets in. This is because they are not used to the new reaction. What

Little Johnny and Little Diana do not realize is that how they reacted five or ten years ago will not apply to how they react now.

That is a wrong experience applied to new experience, which feeds wrong perception. Little Johnny and Little Diana are not with their parents anymore. They are supposed to be adults, and they want all the privileges of an adult—respect, love, care, independence—but not the responsibility. Since they don't want the responsibility of an adult but they want the privileges of it, they live in conflict all the time. What is the conflict? That people don't react to them the way they are used to. They react back; or they don't know how to react or what to do anymore so they show a sour face, they pout, they think "poor me" and they cry. They do nothing. They wait for others to give them a solution because that is what they have expected for years and years and years.

Little Johnny and Little Diana develop a wrong perception of others. They think, "Why are they not doing this for me? I'm a nice person. I acted like this before and my mother and father were nice to me. I am the same person—why am I not getting the same reaction?"

At the same time, another type of wrong perception arises from others back to Little Johnny and Little Diana. Others do not realize that Johnny and Diana had a good life and parents who took wonderful care of them. Instead, they think, "What a selfish, self-centered individual. What a lazy individual. What an unmotivated person. What a loser. I don't want to be around him. I don't want to associate with him." People start to go away from them more and more.

There is wrong perception from the outside of Little Johnny and Little Diana; and wrong perception from them of the outside. It gets bigger. Anger sets in—the anger of not getting what they want and not knowing why.

It is worse when we *do* know why we are not getting what we want, but we are so habituated in our ways that we don't do anything about it. Instead, we run away from situations. Every time a difficult situation comes our way, we run; we can't take it because we are trapped. We have trapped ourselves.

Some people cannot even achieve small things—there's always someone to rescue them or help them. When they grow up, how do they live? They live on wrong experience and wrong perception. The wrong experience is that they've been rescued. The wrong perception is that they still want to live this way and have people take care of them and rescue them. When they live this way, they make people suffer.

When we look back, we may notice that every time we made a little mistake, every time we lost, every time we didn't listen, our daddies and mommies took care of us. If they did that enough times, we grow up to be losers. Whether we stay a loser or not is dependent on our knowledge and our application.

If it took us this much effort to be a loser, that means we *do have effort*. To sit there and wait for years and years for the planet to take care of us is effort. We see everyone moving up, succeeding, getting better and moving to the next level. We see people with bigger cars, nicer bodies, nicer houses, more beautiful wives and husbands. To sit in the middle of everyone moving up and in the middle of all this materialism, and not push ourselves to have anything requires a lot of effort. It is a lot of effort to remain a loser.

Losers, don't think you do not have effort. You *do* have effort. It is just that you don't recognize where you have been dispersing your effort. For losers to stay around and do nothing, not finish their work or their tasks, wait for people to rescue them and just sit there with a "poor me" look takes a lot of work.

When we see homeless people on the streets, there are a few who are genuine, but there are some who are not. It takes a lot of effort to go out there—these people have to overcome their pride, ego and reputation; they have to put up with people looking at them, spitting on them and looking down on them. And it is all for just a few dollars here and there. It is a lot of effort to stay there to maintain that façade.

My point is not to insult losers. My point is that we should recognize how our mind plays tricks on us. We do have effort. If we recognize that we have effort, then we must apply it to something else. We can be an excellent winner just as we can be an excellent loser, because we have the effort.

I go back to my point that if you are born with a lot of wealth and an easy life, if you are used to having things put on a golden platter for you and everything spoon-fed to you, that could be the result of strong negative karma. The wonderful environment makes you not challenge yourself, it makes you not push yourself. It makes you hurt many people around you. If you end up being a loser, you can see that being born into wealth was very bad karma.

Bad karma is not about living on the streets, not having anything, being an orphan or not having money as you were growing up. We read a lot of success stories about people who were on the streets begging, who had no parents, who were refugees, who were maimed or didn't have arms and legs. We also read about a lot of very successful people who came from very successful families.

We also read about very successful families whose children are losers and drug addicts, who are dumb and lazy, waste their life, get fat and just use their parents. And we hear about people who were born on the street or born to parents who were poor and impoverished; they also grow up like that, with their lives impoverished.

Karma is not what you were born into—rich or poor, good or bad. It is the *result* that wealth or poverty brings into your life. In some cases, the poverty and difficulties that people go through as a child make them very strong and powerful as adults. They become very great examples of human beings because of the pain they experienced when they were a child. Some people grow up to continue suffering the pain they experienced and to create pain for others.

For some people, the negative experience of living on the streets is a *result* of positive karma. It is something they prayed for: they prayed to be born into a difficult situation to accelerate their spiritual progress. When they are born into these difficult situations and their story is heard by others when they grow up, it inspires millions.

Some people are born into tremendous wealth. Their mothers and fathers are living Dzambalas, and they were given everything as they were growing up because their parents loved them so much. If they grow up to continue the legacy of their parents' success and kindness, and become successful people in their own right, that can be considered good karma. These people, who are born into very wealthy situations, will use their name, status and position to benefit others, again and again and again. If they grow up to be losers, scared of the world, very naïve, unable to stand on their own, it is not their parents' fault; it is their own "fault," a result of their negative karma, to be born into a situation which does not challenge them.

Don't think that if you have a nice car, a nice apartment and a good life, it is your good luck. It could be bad luck because you will be *using up* all your luck. For people who have expensive cars, expensive houses, expensive clothes, expensive jewellery, expensive lifestyles and everything that is beautiful, the amount of karma they use up every single day to support that lifestyle is tremendous. Therefore, the amount of merit they need to make to support that must be tremendous too.

...Tenacity to Face Ourselves

Once you face yourself, facing everyone else becomes easier.

If we have responsibilities to carry out and work to accomplish, we might run away. When we run away, we think we have escaped, but we have actually opened the door for another negative situation to manifest even more. We don't realize that.

Most people run away from difficult situations. They escape, run away, and think, "I've gotten away with it. I'm alright. See, I made it easy. Everything's alright now." Actually, it is not alright. Situations will become harder and more difficult for people who run away from difficult situations and who don't challenge or push themselves even though they can, until eventually they are unable to handle anything.

Temporarily, we escape from a situation so we don't suffer, or so that we don't have to face any difficulties. We escape because we want to escape from difficulties, yet we invite even more difficulties, in grander, wider and bigger scales.

These difficulties will arise again and again. We may change our whole set of friends, but we are going to have to change them continuously, again and again, or we will have very few friends left! It doesn't mean that people who have very few friends are bad people; it just means they're very narrow-minded or very petty. They look at small things, not at the big things. They create a lot of suffering for themselves and for the people around them.

So how do we deal with these difficulties? What I always say is that confession is very strong because it is to verbalize what we have done. When we confess what we have done, there is no room to hide. When there is no room to hide, it doesn't fester. When it doesn't fester, it doesn't become bigger and bigger and bigger.

When we keep quiet about another person's faults, it is patience, but when we keep quiet about our own faults, it is very damaging. On a psychological level, it is very detrimental. Psychosomatic diseases and problems—which come from the mind—arise from holding, hiding and covering what we have done wrong, and not facing our mistakes.

For some physical ailments, sicknesses and disorders, the source is not really the difficulties we experience externally; the source is from within. Therefore, confession, talking and explaining are very, very powerful methods for overcoming these difficulties. When we do that, we heal psychosomatic disorders.

Some of us may not be convinced about karma and Buddhas, but we can be sure about psychosomatic disorders, which are scientifically proven and treated. These disorders are about hiding something inside until it festers and becomes bigger and bigger, wider and wider. After a long, long time, it becomes very hard for us to escape from it. This comes from running away, avoiding, not facing things and keeping quiet in the hope that everyone will forget... But *we* won't.

When we make mistakes, keep quiet about it and hope that others won't notice, there will be people out there who *won't* notice. But *we* will notice, because we're with ourselves. If we keep quiet about our own mistakes, they will get bigger and they will get stronger. Don't talk about karma. Just talk about psychology.

The secret is not to keep quiet about the wrongs we have done. Isn't that exactly what they teach you in psychology? When you go for therapy, don't they make you open up and talk about the wrongs you have done? Once you can face yourself, facing everyone else becomes easier.

We live with ourselves 24 hours a day. We don't live with others for 24 hours. It's easier to "face" others sometimes because we can avoid them, "turn them off," throw their picture out or not go to the parties they're at. That's easy. But we can't turn ourselves off. We can't avoid ourselves. We can't get away from ourselves. We can't run away from ourselves.

Therefore, we should face ourselves and confess to ourselves first that we are wrong. Then, acknowledging and confessing to someone that can make a difference in our lives—such as a psychologist, teacher, close friend, mentor or parents—is the next step to healing. The healing is to get out of the habit.

27 PEACE GIVES US...

... Wisdom to Overcome Our Mistakes

When we face our mistakes, that mistake will be removed and it will then be replaced with wisdom.

Yes, there are difficult people and complicated people out there and they will do their best to make our lives difficult, but how we react towards them is how much suffering we will create for ourselves. When we react back negatively to others or when we react from a basis that is without any Dharma, we create more harm for ourselves and others.

And these reactions don't ever end. When we retaliate, they'll turn around and retaliate against us. Then we react negatively against them, and they react back negatively to us again. You may ask why *you* should stop; you may think that they should also stop since the reactions come from both sides. But when we know Dharma, when we have come under the grace of Jesus Christ, God or Buddha, or when we have adopted a form of spiritual practice, we should be better than that. Even if we have not adopted a spiritual practice, we still have our family name or a reputation that we should not disgrace. We should consider the people around us—our good countrymen, our families, our husbands and wives—and learn to stop acting in ways that reciprocates harm with harm.

If we are older and more mature, if we have some grey hair on our head, if we have gone through the hard knocks of life and especially if we have learnt some Dharma, we have a very special duty not to react to other people the way they react to us. It takes one person to stand up and say no.

The Buddha does not say that there are no enemies out there and that everything is our fault. No. That is illogical. The Buddha teaches and acknowledges that there *are* enemies, there *are* difficult people and difficult situations, from the time we were born until the time we die, from the people who are the poorest and humblest to the people who are the wealthiest. But he also teaches us that *how we react* determines how much we will suffer from those people or situations.

We cannot change the world and we cannot make the world do or act as we think they should do or act. But we can definitely transform our view and projection of the world. If we change our view and projection of the world, it will be as if the world has changed. Then, whenever someone tries to harm us, we will not harm them back, we will say "I'm sorry" a lot, we will smile and become humble. We will see that their harm will stop. It is not a matter of being right or wrong. It is a matter of stopping harm.

All of us have good points and bad points within us. Sometimes, the bad points take over because of certain situations, people, ways of thinking or habituations that we have developed from the way we grew up. The way we grew up and the way we have encountered things affects us and the way we react to other people.

From these habituations, it sometimes becomes very, very difficult for us to admit our mistakes, to say that we are wrong or to let the other person win. We may think we have won or that we are right when we do not admit our mistake and/or let the other person know that we are wrong. However, we actually create a lot of suffering for ourselves because we then have to constantly cover and explain ourselves. Eventually, no matter how much we explain or talk, our mistakes will be uncovered. And inevitably, we will become unhappy.

We all slip, we all make mistakes and we all do things that we regret later. The key is not to hide our mistakes, to be oblivious to it or try to get away from our mistakes. It is to face them and to make amends with the people who we have hurt and damaged.

Sometimes, we might say that we did not mean to hurt anyone. Yes, most of us do not mean to hurt others but from their perspective, they feel they have been hurt. So if, from their perspective, they have been hurt, we have to ask ourselves what we did, how we acted or what we might have said that has hurt them.

We have to understand that some people may have been shouted at a lot when they were younger and as they were growing up. When we give them even a slightly angry look or we tell them to go away, they might feel very, very hurt because they have experienced that their whole lives. On the other hand, a person who has self-esteem and confidence wouldn't think twice when we shout at them or tell them to go away.

People react differently. From our side, we don't mean any harm or anything bad. No, we don't. But sometimes people may take things wrongly. It is not about forgiveness, or about who is right or wrong. It is about moving on and benefiting others. The issue here is that each one of us is only one person. The others are many. Instead of trying to make others fit into our scheme, thoughts, projections and the way we think things should be, we should try to fit into theirs, especially if we want to practice Dharma.

The real practice of Dharma is not the wealth or physical growth of a Dharma center, or that there are huge crowds of people coming to see your Guru. Anyone can do that—businessmen, conmen, imposters. It doesn't matter if the crowd is big or if the center is large or not. The real growth of a Dharma center is individual students and teachers seeing their mistakes, facing up to their mistakes, and expressing, apologizing and healing.

When people face up to their mistakes and confess, they are not confessing something to their Gurus or to other people. They are confessing to themselves. And when they can confess to themselves and they can face up to their own mistakes, there is growth. Dharma grows when our mind transforms to something much, much better. When our mind improves and faces itself, when we take responsibility for what we are supposed to do and for our emotions, our speech and our mistakes, that is Dharma growth.

Dharma practice is when someone improves their mind, when someone grows and expands. In facing up to their mistakes, it is not that they "lose" or that we "forgive" them. Instead, they actually win—they accept themselves and they grow. And when they grow, the Dharma grows. It takes one person to do this, then another, then another—this is growth.

It is important that when someone makes a mistake, they can face up to it themselves. Telling other people about our mistakes is wonderful but facing up to it ourselves is the best thing we can do. When we face our mistakes, that mistake will be removed and it will then be replaced with wisdom. Then, we are on the road to Enlightenment.

Sometimes, when we admit our mistakes, people may react negatively to us. We may wonder why they are still being nasty to us even though we have already faced up to our mistakes and confessed them. That is not the point. The confession is not about how they react to you. It is about you facing up to what you have done out of your anger, hatred, jealousy or desire.

We all have anger, hatred, jealousy and desire at some point in our lives. When we become angry or jealous, we wish for revenge and fight with others. It's all very good in the moment but what happens when we calm down? Do we want to be accepted back? Do we want people to still love us or do we want to be estranged?

Anger and disharmony are impermanent. Once the anger and disharmony are over, where will we be? That is more important than the moment of anger. When I get angry, I always think, "Do I want to go this far? Do I want to carry it that far? Do I want to do this?" Because I know that by the next day, the next hour or the next minute, my anger will have subsided. When the anger subsides, how will I feel? How will people accept me? Will they feel the same about me or will they lose respect for me?

PART VII

Peace and the Ultimate Reward

Divinity: Developing the Spiritual Heart

When we supress our Divinity, it is us saying, "It doesn't matter how you feel, it is important how I feel. I don't care about you."

To Pray Is to Become Divine

Some religions concentrate on the tradition of making images, *thangkas*,[1] paintings, statues and representations of the enlightened Beings. These practices date back thousands of years and give a lot of people courage and inspiration. Some faiths do not accept any type of holy image. Whichever religious method or practice we choose, they are all valid because they accommodate the needs of different people.

Some people prefer to concentrate on something very powerful and abstract, and they have the ability to do that. Some people would prefer to concentrate on something powerful and non-abstract, something tangible. The bottom line is to hook up to and make a connection to something that is above the ordinary, beyond us, divine. It is us trying to hook up with the Divine and trying to awaken some of that Divinity within us.

Whether you pray to an intangible, all-powerful force or you pray to or solicit something that is tangible, that has a structured form and symbolism, the purpose of both is to become divine and to become closer to Divinity.

To pray, actually, is to become divine.

So if we sit and fold our hands, and we pray to an all-powerful Being, the point of the prayer is to become divine. Becoming divine is not about being able to manifest food where there is no food and raising the dead. It is about the Divinity of human qualities that improve with time.

We should look at and examine ourselves: if we have been praying, making offerings and reciting mantras but we do not see anything divine happening in us, we might question if the Divine really exists, if there is Divinity in us to be tapped, or if we are doing something wrong. Or is it that there is Divinity to be tapped and something divine to propitiate, but we are not running the extra mile to achieve it?

Throughout time, people have had the mistaken view that if they pray or participate in outward rituals—such as bathing the Buddha, making offerings to a holy object, chanting, meditating, or helping a church or a temple—that is divine. However, what I would like to reiterate is that although you are making offerings to the Divine in the hope of becoming closer to the Divine, that is not what Divinity is looking for.

You will not see much difference in the people who only do those outward acts, even after 10, 20 or 30 years of doing them. There are people who have been in Dharma for quite a long time and claim to be Buddhists but you see very little transformation or no change at all in them. In fact, some people degenerate; they go downwards. Is it because the Divine does not exist? Is it because we do not have any Divinity? It cannot be, because it is a human quality to have Divinity.

Here is a clear, logical way to check if you have Divinity within you: if you hear the plight of someone in huge difficulty (such as people living in war-torn countries) or if you hear of people being killed, children being killed or sold into slavery and prostitution, pregnant mothers getting sliced and women being raped, *how do you feel?* Do you cringe? Do you feel uncomfortable? Do you think, "Oh my God, what can I do?" *How* you feel shows that you *do* feel; when you feel, it shows that you have Divinity within you. How much you feel is how much Divinity you have.

What you do upon hearing these things shows how much you put your Divinity into action. If you do not do anything—such as making a devotion or prayer, offering incense or sending donations—you can see your Divinity is there but dormant. It is not active.

Self-Gratification

We will go all the way if it is something for ourselves. For our self-gratification, body-speech-and-mind-gratification, we will go all the way, we will exhaust ourselves, we can stay on for hours and hours, and we can continue to do it year after year after year.

However, in the end, no matter how much we chase to gratify ourselves we will come to a rest, look back and say, "But I'm not gratified. Whatever I've put my energy toward has all blown away in the wind." For all the effort we put in, we feel even more depressed because there has been no result. We may not get the result that we want but we will spend all our time, energy and knowledge on trying to achieve it.

All of us are good at some things that other people are not. This is because we have put time toward these things because we feel that doing it will gratify and bring us happiness. In fact, the more we do it, the more it takes us away. We need to realize that—not as a scolding or put-down, or because we are bad, but as a realisation.

We might pursue self-gratifying pursuits and ignore everything else that is considered holy to our culture. I am not just talking about Buddhism. In some cultures, it is parental care; in other cultures, it is doing community work or meditation. When we self-gratify at the expense of whatever is important in our culture and society, or if we self-gratify at the expense of whatever we are supposed to do, that is where we suppress the Divinity within us. That is where the Divine diminishes.

If we have arrogance or pride and we don't want to share, we don't want to go under it and learn, we are suppressing our Divinity. It is divine to learn. It is divine to improve. But if our ego, our shame or our reputation gets caught, then we are suppressing the Divine.

Divinity or the Divine cannot be damaged in any way. Yet when we go after self-gratification, year after year after year, at the expense of the development and discovery of our Divinity, it is not good. For example, we might write into love columns or personal ads and receive a lot of response. 40 people write back wanting to have sex with us and we feel "happy" because of that. But this type of "happiness" doesn't bring us real happiness. After meeting those 40 people, we think, "Is that all I'm worth? That's it?" Instead, we become more unhappy. We can spend a lot of time writing letters and checking newspapers. We spend hours looking but nothing happens. That takes away from the Divine because it is only self-gratification at the expense of *everything else.*

Self-gratification is not bad; it depends on the amount we pursue and the results we gain from pursuing it. Some of our self-gratification can have beneficial results. For example, someone might be extremely interested in art; he loves to paint and has spent the last 10 years locked up in his room, eating one piece of bread a day and painting, at the expense of his health and friends. He doesn't have anything else. Then, suddenly, he might connect with an organization that asks him to paint for them. His paintings might become a huge success and raise a lot of money for a good cause, such as research for curing cancer. That is wonderful.

But if we are stuck on a self-gratifying activity and we do it just for ourselves, it will take time away from everything and anything that is important.

It is not just Dharma and I am not just talking about going to the Dharma center. People in every country around the world have their own idea of what is important; and individually, everyone has his idea or perception of what should be done.

In Tibetan culture, it is to work part-time for the Dharma, to sincerely donate time and energy to causes related to the Dharma, so that your Gurus, the temple and the Dharma can spread with less hindrance and fewer problems. You don't burden them but you help by taking away the burden. In Chinese society, it might be filial devotion, to take care of your parents. (But you don't go all the way for the wrong purpose—you don't sit there for the rest of your life and not do anything else because you're taking care of your parents. You do it with logic.)

Everyone has his own culture and no one can say one is good or bad because the bottom line is whether we are focusing on what is important or focusing on ourselves. That is the bottom line. That is why there is no argument about what is important in different cultures and in our minds for bringing out our Divinity. All these methods are just vehicles for bringing out our Divinity. It is not the actual action.

In ancient societies and old cultures like the Tibetan, Indian, Japanese or Chinese cultures, our promise and word of honour—or *samaya*[2]—is extremely important. It makes us human or not. It makes us honorable or not. Whatever and whomever we are committed to—whether our Guru is big or small—we must remember what we have promised and do it. That is very precious. If you were to break your promise in ancient Japanese society, you cut your finger off. It is as simple as that. They don't make you do it, but you have to give something back. There is retribution and it shows who you are.

It is very bad when we lose this honor or this statement of who we are because we are suppressing our Divinity. It is us saying, "It doesn't matter how you feel, it is important how I feel. I don't care about you." That is the unspoken message we are giving when we don't do what we are supposed to do, whatever society we are in. People who live like this go further and further down. As the years advance, their reputation, their happiness, what they want and what they pursue will go down, down, down because they are only going after things that suppress the Divine—Buddha-nature, God, Paradise, Heaven, or whatever we want to label it.

Finding Divinity

Whatever society we are in, it is about the same thing: *finding the Divinity within us*. A lot of us have wasted so much time suppressing that Divinity in our self-inflicted world of pain, loneliness and unhappiness, within the borders and barriers we set up. We are so stuck on just *us*.

When you self-gratify, you will burden people with your words, explanations and smiling face. You might be able to get by with your smiling face but it is just a façade. It will end. As time goes by, people will recognize your true nature, who you are and how you are. When they recognize who you are and how you are, and you realize that they have recognized that, you will start to suffer.

When you start to suffer, you can do two things: you can climb out of that suffering and do better, or you can go deeper into it and hide, run away from it, escape, not face it and not improve. If you do the latter, it is only a temporary measure and unfortunately, with all the technology of today—e-mail, communication and telephones—you cannot hide. Now, there are web-cams everywhere, there are nasty people who like to gossip, and who are watching us and reporting on us. Anyway, people are intelligent and educated—they can observe you and surmise what is going on, no matter what your explanations are. There is the ancient proverb of actions speaking louder than words.

Divinity is finding out that you have reached this stage of suppressing the Divine and you *doing something about it*: you go against it and you fight the tide. It is very difficult, it is hard and you may want to give up—but it is easier than running. When you run, you only escape from everyone else, but not from yourself. Wherever you go, who you are will manifest. Your reputation will follow, your habits will follow and how you are will follow. There is no way to escape.

It is not about whether you practice Buddhism deeply, and it is not about whether you do meditations and mantras. If you have a sick father and you don't even go to see him, you are suppressing the Divine. If you do not serve your sick father in any way, you are suppressing the Divine. In your culture, that may be how you manifest your Divinity; you should use that as a vehicle to manifest the Divine.

What is divine? Something which is divine is all-encompassing. It is harmony. It is making another being feel good. It is us feeling good as a result of making another being feel happy and relieving him of his suffering. It is divine to be alert and awake, especially to people's needs.

When we give people whatever they need or want, when we do whatever we can do to help and relieve them of their suffering, and when we are aware, that is divine. The Divine is improvement within ourselves, opening up, developing more awareness and relieving other people of their suffering. And as the years go by, we will see ourselves opening up, not running away, not hiding, not getting deeper into our self-gratifications and having everything else thrown to the wind.

GLOSSARY

Avalokiteshvara—Buddha of Compassion. Also known as Chenrezig (Tibetan) and Kuan Yin (Chinese).

Bodhisattva—an enlightened Being that keeps returning into our world to show us the path to happiness.

Buddha—an enlightened Being. This does not only refer to Beings in the Buddhist tradition, but to anyone who has attained Enlightenment.

butterlamps—traditionally, candles in Tibet were made of yak butter. As butter was quite hard to come by, offering butterlamps on the altar was considered a very precious offering. Nowadays, we may offer candles, but the traditional containers which hold the candles are still referred to as butterlamps.

Dakinis—literally, "Sky Walkers" or "Sky Go-ers" in Tibetan. *Dakinis* refers to enlightened, celestial Beings and highly spiritual women.

Dharma—this is loosely translated as "truth" or "right conduct." Dharma does not refer just to Buddhist teachings but emphasizes right conduct or a right path for attaining permanent happiness for ourselves and others.

Dharma Protector—Protectors are celestial beings that emanate in a form that specifically helps to clear obstacles to our spiritual practice.

divination—in a Buddhist context, this is a highly developed method of assessing someone's karmic situation and receiving beneficial advice directly from enlightened Beings.

Dzambala—Buddha of Generosity and Inner and Outer Wealth (physical, financial wealth and spiritual growth).

Heruka—a tantric form of the Buddha Avalokiteshvara.

ignorance—ignorance in Buddhist teachings does not refer to what is commonly regarded as "stupidity." It is a term used to describe our clinging on to limited and often false concepts which lead to developing strong aversions and attachments. This, in turn, leads to engaging in actions that bring us unhappiness.

Guru—in Buddhism, this refers to our spiritual teacher or guide.

initiations—the empowerment and permission to engage in certain advanced religious practices.

karma—Sanskrit for "action." *Karma* refers to the universal law of cause and effect, where every physical, verbal and mental action (positive, negative and neutral) creates a corresponding reaction.

Lama—in Buddhism, this refers to our spiritual teacher or guide. (See also **Guru**)

mantras—mystic formulas that contain the spiritual energy of the Buddhas in the form of sound. Reciting mantras invokes these enlightened energies within us.

merits—positive potential that is gained from selfless, virtuous actions, speech and thoughts. Merit supports and leads us further on our spiritual path and attainments.

offerings—we make offerings of the best materials we can afford to the Three Jewels as a way to collect merit to support our spiritual practice. By making offerings to an enlightened Being, we are effectively making a prayer to attain the qualities they embody. Examples of offerings are flowers, light (candles), incense, water, food, or precious items like silver or jewels, etc.

preliminary practice—these practices set the foundation for us to advance to higher teachings and practices. The preliminary practices include 100,000 each of 1) Prostrations, 2) Vajrasattva mantras, 3) Mandala offerings, 4) Guru Yoga practice and 5) Water bowl offerings.

refuge—submitting oneself fully with total faith and trust to one's Guru and to the power of the Three Jewels to teach and help us traverse the path to Enlightenment.

Rinpoche—greatly precious one. Respectful and loving way to address a highly attained spiritual teacher.

Sadhana—prayers and meditations that are done on a regular, daily basis.

Samaya—the sacred bond and commitment to one's spiritual teacher, based on strong faith, devotion and effort. With this commitment, we are propelled forward exponentially in the spiritual practices and work we do.

Samsara—the cycle of existence where beings continue to create and experience their own sufferings, lifetime after lifetime.

Sangha—this refers to the pantheon of all enlightened Beings and to monastic communities. Generally, the Sangha are all practitioners of the Buddhist path.

self-cherishing mind—the mind that regards itself as wholly important and puts itself first. It is a mind that views itself as independently existing, and therefore reacts to protect and look after itself exclusively, disregarding the needs of all those around it.

Shakyamuni—the historical sage, Lord Buddha, who set down the liberating teachings 2,500 years ago that we continue to follow today.

stupa—a structure that represents the enlightened mind. Also known as *pagoda* in some countries.

Tantra/tantric practice—the practice of taking the result onto the path where we identify with and work directly with the energies and qualities of an enlightened Being instead of our limited concepts of ourselves.

Tara—a female Buddha who manifests in 21 forms.

Thangka—traditional Tibetan art depicting deities and enlightened Masters.

Three Jewels—the Buddha, Dharma and Sangha.

three lower realms—the animal, spirit and hell realms.

(Lama/Je) Tsongkhapa—one of Buddhism's most prominent enlightened Masters from the 14th Century, who was especially known for his ardent study, practice and teaching of the Dharma. Lama Tsongkhapa fully embodies three great *Bodhisattvas*—Avalokiteshvara (Buddha of Compassion), Manjushri (Buddha of Wisdom) and Vajrapani (Buddha of Spiritual Power).

Vajrayogini—a tantric female Buddha who embodies the essence of wisdom and compassion.

Vipassana—an ancient meditation technique dating back to Buddha Shakyamuni that focuses on developing and training in awareness.

Yidam—a meditational deity (such as Tara or Vajrayogini) upon whom practitioners focus to attain their enlightened qualities.

CHAPTER NOTES

Chapter 1

1. The term *Dharma* carries many levels of meaning. At the most basic level, it can be translated as "right conduct"—seeing, thinking, feeling, speaking and acting in ways conducive to lasting happiness, peace and benefit for ourselves and others. *Dharma* often refers to the teachings that were given by the historical sage, Buddha Shakyamuni, 2,500 years ago. However, this is not restricted to Buddhism or Buddhist teachings. We can also refer to Christian Dharma, Hindu Dharma, etc., and to all teachings that promote these same messages of peace and altruism.

2. *Karma* is a Sanskrit word meaning "action" and refers to the universal law of cause and effect. This means that every action of our body, speech and mind—whether positive, negative or neutral—generates a corresponding reaction or result.

3. A group of words or syllables likened to prayers which are recited out loud. Mantras embody the energies of the Buddhas in the form of sound and are believed to invoke the blessings of enlightened Beings.

Chapter 2

1. To engage in a retreat is to enter seclusion for a period of time to focus on meditation, prayers or specific practices that are advised by a spiritual guide or teacher.

2. Three years, three months and three days is the time period for a traditional, long retreat.

Chapter 3

1. Literally, *dakinis* means "sky walkers" or "sky go-ers" in Tibetan and refers to female celestial beings.

2. Vajrayogini is one of the highest female tantric Buddhas.

3. Tara is one of the most popular female Buddhas in the Tibetan pantheon.

4. *Sex* is not a term that is appropriate for a Tibetan Lama to mention publicly. Tsem Rinpoche came

up with the term "boobali" as a substitute...which always makes for much laughter!

5. A compilation of prayers that are recited on a daily basis.

6. Heruka is the consort of Vajrayogini; also one of the highest tantric Buddhas.

7. The Tibetan word for a spiritual teacher or spiritual guide. "Lama" is often used interchangeably with "Guru," which is the Sanskrit equivalent.

8. Meditational deities which practitioners base their meditations and practices on.

Chapter 4

1. *Samsara* is the cycle of existence where sentient beings continue to create and experience their own suffering, lifetime after lifetime.

2. One of the most famous Buddhist mantras. It is the mantra of the Buddha of Compassion, known as Avalokiteshvara or Chenrezig. See pp. 95–96 for a more detailed explanation.

3. Positive energy generated by our virtuous thoughts, actions and speech which helps to propel us further in our spiritual practices.

Chapter 6

1. Kuan Yin is the Chinese name for the Buddha of Compassion. Also known as Chenrezig (in Tibetan) or Avalokiteshvara (in Sanskrit).

2. Lama Tsongkhapa is the 14th century Buddhist scholar and saint who founded the Gelugpa school of Buddhism.

3. Dzambala is the Buddha of Inner and Outer Wealth.

Chapter 7

1. An ancient meditation technique dating back to Buddha Shakyamuni that focuses on developing and training in awareness.

Chapter 8

1. Prostrations and water offerings are physical practices that aid in meditation and contemplation, and are very central to Buddhist practice.

Chapter 9

1. A prayer written by the Tibetan Buddhist Master Geshe Langri Tangpa, which presents the essence of all mind- or thought-transformation (*lojong*) teachings.

Chapter 13

1. The central belief of reincarnation in Buddhism states that any of us can be reborn in any of the six realms of existence (hell, spirits, animals, humans, demi-gods or gods). The conditions into which we are reborn are determined and driven

by our karma, which we are creating at every moment of our lives.

Chapter 14

1. *"Om...Hung Phet"* is commonly recited in many mantras and prayers; these three syllables are often arranged in this particular order with other syllables in between. For example: Om Kalarupa Hung Phet. Rinpoche makes a witty play on words here.

Chapter 15

1. At the age of 7, Tsem Rinpoche was given up for adoption to a Mongolian foster family in New Jersey, America. There, he suffered tremendous physical and emotional abuse regularly from his foster mother, who was later diagnosed to have been suffering from schizophrenia. At 16, Rinpoche ran away from home and hitchhiked across the United States to Los Angeles, California, where he found a safe refuge in Thubten Dhargye Ling Dharma center, studying under the great Buddhist Master from Gaden Shartse Monastery, Geshe Tsultim Gyeltsen.

Chapter 18

1. Rinpoche refers here to his birth father. From a very young age, Rinpoche was given up for adoption, first to a Taiwanese family in Taipei, Taiwan,

and later to a Mongolian foster family in New Jersey, USA. He did not have the opportunity to meet his birth father until he was in his 20s.

Chapter 20

1. Shantideva's ground-breaking treatise on the cultivation of great compassion, called *The Bodhisattva's Way of Life*.

Chapter 21

1. A highly developed method of assessing someone's karmic situation and receiving beneficial advice directly from enlightened Beings.

Chapter 22

1. This refers to the three lower realms of existence: hell, spirit realms, or being reborn as an animal. The three higher realms refer to the human realm and the realms of demi-gods and gods. These six realms constitute *samsara*.

Chapter 24

1. Happy New Year wishes in Mandarin.

Chapter 28

1. *Thangkas* are traditional Tibetan paintings, usually of Buddhist deities.

2. *Samaya* is a Tibetan word which means the sacred bond and commitment to one's spiritual teacher, based on strong faith, devotion and effort.

KECHARA

Established in 2000, Kechara is a non-profit Buddhist organization under the spiritual guidance of His Eminence Tsem Rinpoche. It is an affiliate of the illustrious 600-year-old Gaden Shartse Monastery, which is now situated in Mundgod, South India. Gaden Shartse Monastery belongs to the holy Gaden Monastery which now houses more than 3,000 monks and is regarded as one of the most elite monastic universities in the world.

The Kechara organization seeks to bring the beautiful, ancient wisdom of Buddhism to as many people as possible around the world. It offers a range of programs that include introductory classes on Buddhism, prayer sessions and wonderful opportunities to volunteer in Buddhist-related arts, publishing and community service.

While based in Malaysia and Nepal, Kechara also has supporters and friends from all around the world who follow its activities via its Website and online social network. Since its inception, Kechara has grown into several departments:

Tsem Ladrang—the private residence and office of H.E. Tsem Rinpoche; also the headquarters of the Kechara organization.

Kechara House—the main Dharma center which is based on the outskirts of Kuala Lumpur, Malaysia.

Kechara Care—an information and visitors' center for the organization.

Kechara Discovery—a travel consultancy which organises pilgrimages to holy places and sources for statues to complement the selection at the outlets.

Kechara Forest Retreat—A unique holistic retreat center focused on the total wellness of body, mind and spirit in a natural forest environment.

Kechara InMotion—a film production house.

Kechara Lounge—an information center and lounge overlooking the Boudhanath Stupa in Kathmandu, Nepal.

Kechara Media & Publications—the publishing arm.

Kechara Oasis—new-age vegetarian restaurants.

Kechara Paradise—retail outlets in prominent areas of Kuala Lumpur and Penang, offering handicrafts and artifacts from the Himalayan region.

Kechara Saraswati Arts—the first Himalayan arts studio in Southeast Asia.

Kechara Soup Kitchen—a community action group which distributes food to the homeless and urban poor in Malaysia.

Kechara World Peace Centre—the future spiritual sanctuary and alternative arts, healing and philosophy center in Malaysia.

If you would like to know more about Kechara, please contact us at:

**Kechara House
No. 7, Jalan PJU 1/3G,
SunwayMas Commercial Centre,
47301 Petaling Jaya,
Selangor, Malaysia**

Kechara Media & Publications

Kechara Media & Publications (KMP) is a not-for-profit publishing arm of the Kechara Buddhist Organization. First established in 2005 by a group of young and dedicated students, KMP's vision is to bring H.E. Tsem Rinpoche's teachings and the ancient wisdom of Dharma into the context of contemporary living.

KMP also publishes inspirational, motivational books by His Eminence's students, who are talented up-and-coming authors equally committed to bringing this message of peace and wisdom to others. To reach as wide an audience as possible, KMP produces books in English and Chinese that are retailed in the Kechara Dharma stores, leading bookshops and online.

Our work is really a labor of love

All sponsorships are invaluable to us, as it helps us to continue publishing books that inspire and transform people's minds. We believe that by sponsoring our books, you are directly and actively helping others to connect to this wisdom energy, to gain happiness and peace of mind. You also create the cause to gain tremendous wisdom for yourself, to be able to bring positive change for the betterment of your life and the lives of your loved ones.

By our books, we hope that reading will serve as a powerful and inspiring method for healing and mind transformation—creating a shift from negative ways of thinking, to positive, altruistic and compassionate attitudes. By giving new perspectives and bringing peace through our books, many more people will not only reach out with heartfelt sincerity to help the homeless, abused children and victims of natural disasters but more importantly, be closer, kinder, more compassionate and patient with their families, colleagues, loved ones and society at large. Only through this can we create the causes for Inner Peace and Outer Peace, and eventually World Peace may become a reality.

Thank you for your support of KMP's cause of healing through reading.

For more information about KMP, please contact us at:

Kechara Media & Publications Sdn. Bhd.
No. 41-2A & 41-2B, 1st Floor
Jalan PJU 1/3C, SunwayMas Commercial Centre,
47301 Petaling Jaya,
Selangor, Malaysia
Tel: (+603) 7805 5691
E-mail: kmp@kechara.com
Fax: (+603) 7805 5690
Website: *www.kechara.com/kmp*

We also welcome volunteers to assist with transcribing, translation, editing or graphic design. If you are interested in joining us or in contributing in any way towards the production of books, DVDs and online teachings, please contact us, no matter where you are in the world. We would love to have you on board!

Kechara Forest Retreat: Creating Conscious Communities

In the heart of Bentong, Malaysia is a 35-acre retreat center like no other in this region. Set in the midst of lush tropical forest is the Kechara Forest Retreat, a place designed to develop a perfect balance of total wellness—body, mind and spirit. Offering comfortable accommodation, extensive facilities and the promise of peace and tranquility, this is the perfect destination for the spiritual at heart.

Conceptualized by H.E. Tsem Rinpoche as the heart of the Kechara organization, our mission is to have those who walk through our gates experience a sustainable spiritual lifestyle that will leave mind and body rejuvenated and inspired.

We offer wholesome activities to help families and friends bond meaningfully, the weary find inner peace and the perfect getaway to find oneself and inspiration.

We believe in giving back to society through educational programs for the young and old, instilling universal positive values such as patience, tolerance, mindfulness and compassion. It is our fondest wish that all who walk through our doors return home inspired, sharing what they have learnt within their own communities, thus creating a global revolution of consciousness and kindness.

For more information and latest updates, please go to *retreat.kechara.com*.

We would love to hear from you. Please contact us for any enquiries about Kechara Forest Retreat, activities and sponsorship opportunities.

Tel. No.: +603 78033908, Email: retreat@kechara.com